Spirituality God's Rx for Stress

Spirituality
God's Rx
for Stress

60 Ways to Get Your Soul in Shape

NEIL B. WISEMAN

Beacon Hill Press of Kansas City
Kansas City, Missouri

Copyright 1992
by Beacon Hill Press of Kansas City

ISBN: 083-411-4291

Printed in the
United States of America

Unless otherwise indicated all Scripture quotations are from *The Holy Bible, New International Version* (NIV), copyright © 1973, 1978, 1984 by the International Bible Society, and are used by permission of Zondervan Bible Publishers.

Permission to quote from other copyrighted versions of the Bible is acknowledged with appreciation:

The Bible: An American Translation (Goodspeed), by J. M. Powis Smith and Edgar J. Goodspeed. Copyright 1923, 1927, 1948 by the University of Chicago Press.

The *New English Bible* (NEB), © The Delegates of the Oxford University Press and The Syndics of the Cambridge University Press, 1961, 1970.

The *New King James Version* (NJKV), copyright © 1979, 1980, 1982, Thomas Nelson, Inc., Publishers.

The New Testament in Modern English (Phillips), Revised Edition © J. B. Phillips, 1958, 1960, 1972. By permission of the Macmillan Publishing Co.

The *Revised Standard Version of the Bible* (RSV), copyright 1946, 1952, © 1971, 1973.

The Living Bible (TLB), © 1971 by Tyndale House Publishers, Wheaton, Ill.

King James Version (KJV).

Contents

Introduction	7
Spirituality and Stress Are Real	
1. Spirituality—Putting Life in Balance	13
2. Spirituality—Markers for the Journey	31
3. Stress—Disenchantment with the Substitutes	45
4. Hunger for the Holy	59
Remedies for Stress	
5. Cultivate the Center	75
6. Sing Your Stress Away	93
7. Make Time Your Friend	115
8. Cherish Relationships	139
9. Pray Change into Your Life	165
10. Follow the Manufacturer's Manual	191
Exercises to Strengthen the Heart	
11. Exercises to Make Your Heart like His	215
Epilogue	241
Notes	243

Introduction

You are not alone. Everyone battles stress—some of us more regularly than others. Stess is difficult to escape because it is so deeply rooted in our overstuffed lives. Debilitating symptoms stalk us: fatigue, hopelessness, detachment, boredom, self-pity, depression, even suicidal thoughts or a variety of physical complaints. Stress drains our energies and spoils our quality of life.

But spirituality, a miraculous cure for stress, is available to everyone.

Spiritual development provides coping skills, so that we are not victimized by frightening circumstances or imprisoning expectations of others.

What is spirituality? Let's call it an inner strength for dealing with external pressures.

Spirituality fulfills our need for God, which endless rounds of possessions, projects, or even interesting people will never satisfy. Such a deepening friendship with God toughens the inner immune system against hurry sickness.

Whatever your milepost of life, spirituality stands ready to remedy stress. Think of the liberating possibilities:

Working mother, you need not be pressured by conflicts between home and job. Minute-by-minute contact with the Inner Calm is yours for the asking.

Senior adult, you have help for your fear of the future as you organize your life around Christ, the Center.

Young professional, your job tensions can be significantly reduced. Silent strength is available from the Inner Spring.

Empty nester, there is no need to float along on a bewildering sea of mid-life frustrations. The Father wants you to find meaning in friendship with Him.

Single parent, you need not be confused by lonely child-rearing tasks, complicated by limited funds and time. The Inner Compass points you to the Father.

Tense businessperson, give up brooding about shrinking profits, long hours, and hostile takeovers. The Enabler offers to be your silent Partner.

Christian worker, yield your spiritual dryness to God. The Strengthener goes before you into every task you attempt for Christ.

This book shares my own amazing discoveries that spiritual development heals stress. As I wrote, I kept learning new ways about how God makes robust adventures of wholeness, wellness, and holiness available to every hungry soul. Contemporary pilgrims and ancient masters join me in these pages to offer time-tested strategies to all who want to get their soul in shape.

In these heart-to-heart conversations, secularists will find the missing ingredients they seek for a satisfying life; recent converts will be shown how to add joy to their journey with the living Lord; and veteran sojourners will be challenged by forgotten or neglected treasures. All seekers, regardless of their stage in life, can deepen their intimacy with Christ.

Chapters 5 through 10 each offer 10 spiritual development exercises to translate the concepts of spirituality into authentic flesh-and-blood realities. These exercises help readers apply the strengths of spirituality to the tiniest details of their pilgrimage.

Throughout this writing process, many soul friends have been stimulating companions. I remembered, as I wrote, times in other days when they raised pressing questions. I drew strength from the silent support of others. Though many friends are affectionately introduced through the book, I am indebted to hundreds of unnamed persons. I cherish every influence; my gratitude is great to many.

Special thanks to Bonnie, my wife, lover, and affirming critic; to Betty, my longtime secretary who typed this manuscript more times than either of us cares to count; to Audrey, my second mother in the faith, who offered suggestions and taught me many lessons about the inner quest; and to J. Fred, encouraging literary consultant.

Grace and peace to friends in the Pompano Beach, Fla., congregation who lived much of the book with me while I was their pastor; our relationship as fellow strugglers after God is among the most precious joys of my life. I also owe spiritual and emotional debts to my parents, Neil A. and Marguerite Wiseman, and to my grown children, Scott, Todd, and Carla.

An affirming "straight ahead" to all who seek soul health. God awaits your permission to satisfy your thirst and transform your hunger into spiritual fatness. Sing with me, in James Nicholson's words, "Lord Jesus, I long to be perfectly whole; I want Thee forever to live in my soul."

—NEIL B. WISEMAN

Spirituality and Stress Are Real

> "Do you want to be whole?"
> —Jesus of Nazareth

1

SPIRITUALITY— PUTTING LIFE IN BALANCE

Dummy, can't you see the mountains are too #*#*#*#* big for one picture?" That's how an Archie Bunker-type tourist evaluated his picture-taking efforts in the Rocky Mountains. Stubbornly his wife coaxed him to pose in front of the mountains as she tried to capture an Alpine scene to show her friends back home. After several attempts she gave up. "I can't do it either. The Rockies are too big for my camera." She was right; such spectacular beauty can never be captured in a single photograph.

This frustration occurs often in the mountains. Most tourists, soon after arriving in the Rockies, grab a camera to photograph the awesome peaks, but the results are generally disappointing. Even the most gifted professional photographers and talented painters experience this difficulty. Clearly, the magnificent Rockies must be experienced firsthand. The morning moods, the midday brilliance, or the evening shadows are too majestic to be duplicated on film or painted on canvas.

To develop even a casual acquaintance with the mountains takes exhilarating efforts like spring walks through flower-carpeted meadows, hikes up barren summer peaks, brisk visits to autumn aspen groves, and bone-chilling exposure to snow showers. The rewards, however, make the effort worthwhile. Such rugged beauty draws people back again and again; some call it a lifelong love affair.

More subtle and significant, but on a deeper level, intimacy with God is even more difficult to describe. From the beginning of time, gifted writers and ordinary disciples have felt thwarted in their attempts to use Christianity as a lens for clarifying life. Words, however, are feebly anemic as we try to explain how faith heals the soul or why God confronts us when we stray from the path home. Songs and poems—inspiring though they may be—are too small to express the wonder. And to these difficulties of expression pivotal questions must be added: Who knows why spirituality produces purpose for life? Who understands the mysteries that permeate everything? Or, who can explain why a satisfying life of faith does not rely on logic alone?

In mountain climbing, the pure high country air makes climbers feel alive, even exuberant. But something more compelling surprises hikers on the spiritual journey. It is the indescribable Presence. That wonderful Someone meets us frequently and intensely in the peaks of spiritual formation. This near side of God, as the first step in spiritual development, challenges us to give wholehearted attention to our neglected inner world. As a result, even a brief meeting with Him inspires us to think more clearly, love more deeply, and live more nobly. When that happens, a memory of incredible meaning is formed in us—a time when we are awestruck by the holy awareness that God belongs to us and we belong to Him.

Seekers in this faith journey soon discover that each new vista is alive with the presence of God, like the holy ground in the experience of Moses. This indescribable Mystery attracts sojourners to new heights of faith formation, lights secularized darkness, and reminds us that tarrying on the plateaus only delays the next discovery. God challenges us to keep climbing, sometimes almost dragging us to new heights. Clearly, no one climbs the faith formation peaks alone; like a worried mother or concerned father, God follows us and finds us wherever we are.

Lessons from the peaks of spirituality seep gently into the soul, so that we expect adventure in the next height and find purpose in the last valley.

Spirituality Has Many Names and Faces

Spirituality, a magnificently rich word, is often misused as a label for mysticism, legalism, or religious highs. Some think, with good reason, the word describes saints who have become walking examples of old-fashioned muddleheadedness. Others think spirituality describes pious robot-types who are arrogant scolds with a perpetual frown. For others spirituality connotes a sickeningly sweet frosting on the human experience, which is reserved for naive supersaints. No wonder spirituality gets laughed out of life as insignificant and irrelevant.

For all these reasons and more, some religious leaders teach or imply that faith formation is a harmless idiosyncrasy but not as substantial as correct doctrine or social activism. As a result, many contemporary Christians consider spirituality to be a hard-to-understand stepchild. But stability of the soul is God's remedy for stress-producing blandness, treacherous double-dealing, religious masquerading, or smoldering cynicism.

The literature of spirituality, when carefully read, destroys many myths about superficial religion by providing vividly descriptive names for faith formation. These titles help explain how spirituality rescues moderns from stress-causing merry-go-rounds. These descriptions open an incredible number of authentic insights to help pilgrims understand how God heals tensions, quiets anxieties, and creates a holy thirst for himself.

A mere reading of the titles strengthens the soul. Each description puts us on a trail of meaning. Such a discovery prompted one writer to summarize spirituality as the God-given capacity for relationships with himself. Nouwen, the Catholic devotional writer, calls spirituality "a burning desire to be forever united with God."[1] Deep down, everyone needs such a connection with the Father so that they can see significance in everything—victories, failures, dreams, and disappointments.

Writers from various traditions describe this Godward quest with phrases like in-Christness, a God-seeker, intimacy with Christ, inner spring, a place of stillness, a richness not impoverished by circumstances, the Center, hunger of the heart, Christ-shaped wholeness, and the Christ life. At its heart, spirituality means paying careful attention to God.

Other soul-stretching synonyms include a holy balance, a quest for spiritual vitality, harmony with God, the divine mystery, a longing for servitude to the Savior, wistfulness for lost communion, a Christ-centered core of character, and an invitation to pilgrimage. These captivating word pictures lead us to a convincing conclusion that spirituality makes intimacy with God possible.

When taken together, these vivid titles describe how spiritual development liberates us from purposelessness and helps us see that much of modern stress is really a spiritual struggle.

Spirituality Creates Inquisitiveness

Spirituality begins with an intense curiosity to know God better. This inquisitive attraction, the opposite of stupefying aimlessness, was explained by Henry H. Williams, Sen. Sam Ervin, Jr.'s, professor at the University of North Carolina: "A man's life seeks God for the same reason that water seeks the ocean. That is where it came from."[2] This search for significance, much more than a search for mere information, leads to the Source who aches for every lost son or daughter to come home.

Simply stated, spirituality satisfies the ravenous inner hunger for completeness that every human being feels. It answers the ultimate questions asked by tycoons on Wall Street and yuppies in suburbia. Even when superficial religion has grown stone cold, spirituality pursues us like the poet's Hound of Heaven down dead-end streets of ignorant faithlessness and arrogant willfulness.

Faith development answers the misgiving of the hillbilly who went to hear the new preacher's first sermon. The beginning minister, a recent graduate of a prestigious New England seminary, had recently moved to a small Appalachian church. After hearing the polished sermon, the mountaineer commented, "I believe he can think, but does he know how to live and can he feel anything?" All dimensions of life—thought, character, and feeling—are nourished by an inquisitive quest for God. The possibilities are limitless because we discover something new each day.

Spiritual formation, because it cherishes systemized thought and doctrinal fidelity, welcomes the scrutiny of razor-sharp minds. But spirituality is more than strenuous intellectual activity or well-organized theology. Fully as much as a way of thinking, it is a way of living. Its main concerns are inner connections like belonging and becoming. It seeks to understand how faith shapes persons, movements, and nations. Spirituality, as it adds balance and color to life, motivates persons to volunteer to be bondslaves to Jesus. This inner-life development heals moral agonies and unshackles broken dreams.

Spirituality impacts life. It is more than a scholar's theory, a saint's rhetoric, or a believer's notion. Spirituality means living with Christ at the center of human existence, a connection at the core of character between God and us.

Spiritual development is like a first-time traveler in a new country who notices simple things like uprooted trees, weathered signs, or strange architecture. A similar response happens in the spiritually awakened struggler. Interest in spirituality increases with each new discovery. Then, our inner sight changes irrevocably, so we start seeing God in unexpected places like an old man's toothless smile, or a pile of autumn leaves. C. S. Lewis said, "One who has journeyed into a strange land cannot return unchanged."[3] This developing vision causes us to see God everywhere we look. Consequently, everything a person learns about the Father intensifies his desire to know more.

Spirituality Invigorates Life

Spirituality nourishes an eagerness to be what God calls us to be. At the same time, authentic spirituality provides a necessary corrective for the past and insightful direction for the future. This correction insists that God no longer be boxed up in the church, the Bible, or prayer. This directive for the future takes faith into life—including secularized places.

When this happens, spirituality no longer runs alongside life, but it reconnects the human journey to God. It allows the supernatural to become a central force in life. Like an inner gravity, faith formation draws everything Godward; inwardly we pray and worship, but outwardly we work and serve.

Even though spirituality may not be fully understood, it intensifies the haunting in our soul for a balanced life. This symmetry in the inner world offers alternatives to the restlessness produced by secularized living even as it replaces boredom caused by mere gentility. Then stress goes down to manageable levels as revolutionary ways of thinking and behaving open to us. In the process, divine unexpectedness surprises us, so that we never know what situation or guise will put us in touch with God.

Like climbing the incredible Rockies, memories of past spiritual growth draws sojourners back again and again to the Source. Happy remembrances of adventures along the trail, challenging visions at the peak, or life-enriching solutions in the valley make the attraction nearly irresistible. Every satisfying climb deepens our inner desire to explore new peaks of devotion. Then discomfort caused by earlier workouts seems dim, even unimportant.

Spirituality is a rhythm of the soul that moves between a struggle to be like Christ and the soul at rest in grace.

Spirituality Promises Meaning

No one completely escapes a gnawing God-hunger. Like salt makes the body crave water, our interior emptiness makes us thirst for ways to face a thousand stress issues that may be as diverse as bitter disappointments, world poverty, and conflicting ideologies. This thirst for meaning makes us understand the society matron's true-to-life dissatisfaction: "Before I met Christ, my outer life was all shine, and my inner life was all sham."

During a similar search, Augustine prayed centuries ago, "Thou hast made us for thyself, O Lord; and our heart is restless until it rests in thee."[4] The Psalmist, years before the New Testament was written, wistfully sang, "As the deer pants for streams of water, so my soul pants for you, O God" (42:1). And because we are God-starved, too, in Christ we seek for answers about meaning, and we are not disappointed.

Spirituality, to fill our emptiness, suggests we blend old basics with new discoveries. Just as a study of the ocean starts with tide tables and temperatures, spirituality starts with Scripture and prayer. But it takes more than tide tables and temperatures to know the ocean; each time casual observers or trained specialists go to the sea, they discover something intriguingly new about its quiet power, noble beauty, and incredible vastness. Spiritual formation is like that. Something excitingly old and something incredibly new is formed in us each time we come near Jesus.

As a result, Christ, the energizing Center of life, gives

pilgrims a satisfying personal identity and a reason for living. One theologian calls it a quest for "the God who has authorized the search and evoked the yearning." This happens as spirituality infuses tired religious ideas with fresh meaning; the result is a double-edged hunger and fullness, want and plenty, poverty and abundance, quest and satisfaction, search and security. These longings form the foundation for a satisfying life, so that the more we learn about God, the more we want to know.

Though the search provides a welcome oasis in a stress-filled world, it requires massive interior renovation and extensive outward changes. Few people make such adjustments easily or comfortably. But should the process seem painful, we can take heart because we know our most crippling stress will be relieved as God shatters our superficial preoccupations and pushes us to honest engagement with himself.

Spirituality forces us to take charge of everything inside our skin—feeling, will, faith, intellect, and physical well-being. Without faith for integration, these forces keep us running a mad dash to nowhere, keeping life superficial. But spiritual formation nurtures wholeness by clearing stress from our minds and souls.

Spirituality Changes Character and Culture

Spirituality, or its lack, shapes many dimensions of human life. The American philosopher William James observed, "We and God have business with each other; and in opening ourselves to His influence, our deepest destiny is fulfilled."[5]

A persistent question remains about spiritual revolutions in society: Is spiritual formation personal and private, or is it worldly and social?

Spirituality is both personal and public. Service is the way it moves from the inner to the outer world. Then, in its finest hour, spiritual formation energizes society and church. Both are transformed by individuals who have experienced a personal faith that revolutionized them forever. As a result, these persons make such a profound impact on society that, according to Scripture, the world is not worthy of them and cannot repay its debt to them. (See Heb. 11:38.) Spirituality, both private and social, always starts with Christ; to love God is to care deeply for His world.

Albert Day, in his *Autobiography of Prayer,* correctly views personal piety as a force to change society: "Religion is not a mere recipe for the malaise of the individual self. It should be a redemptive force in society. It is a summons to heroic, self-forgetful crusades for a better world. It is a demand for, and an investment with, those concerns for society that may cost a man not only his ease but his life."[6] History supports Day's compelling argument that spiritual revolutions often start with a single transformed person. The long list includes Luther, Wesley, Moody, Graham, and thousands of unknown Christian revolutionaries. To the question, if improvements in society do not begin with a single person, where does righteous action start? Karl Barth shines this light: "To clasp the hands in prayer is the beginning of an uprising against the disorder of the world."[7]

Only persons made over by God can change the world and renew the church. An abundantly resourced inner world sends them out to establish justice, mercy, and peace in place of hatred, fear, and conflict. The raw materials for such a transformation include conversion, renewal, purity, and selflessness. These components make reconciliation possible on three levels: with God, with other human beings, and with self. Spirituality, which begins in the individual, quickly expands into a driving force to make persons and groups think and act Christianly in the world. Genuine personal piety and the pain of the world meet in a spiritually responsive person; it is easy to observe Dag

Hammarskjöld's summary at work: "In our era, the road to holiness necessarily passes through the world of action."[8]

Spirituality Produces Wholeness

Spirituality offers inner wellness because it provides healing for everything from minor spiritual upsets to the destructive cancer of doubt. The importance of wholeness is spelled out on a prominent placard at the United States Air Force Academy near Colorado Springs: "The body needs exercise to develop strength and fitness. The mind must be challenged to develop the intellect. But for a person to be truly integrated, the spirit must also grow." God etches, as we have already seen, a hunger for himself on every soul that no amount of success or stress can erase. Malcolm Muggeridge is right: "To look for God is to find Him, and having found Him, we can never again be permanently separated."[9] He never leaves us even when we try to desert Him.

Ideas about connections between body, mind, and soul began appearing in psychological, medical, and religious journals in the 1960s. Based on this expanding knowledge, researchers from many fields began to agree that mind, body, emotions, and spirit are linked together like a string of Christmas tree lights. Every facet of human existence interacts with every other aspect of life—a convincing reason to pursue interior wholeness.

When one considers these findings, it is easy to understand why fragmented treatments cannot heal sicknesses of the soul. Consequently, an old but apparently new solution must be applied to life. The Swiss psychiatrist Paul Tournier states what others said before and are now saying after him, "The doctors seek to help the whole by healing the parts, whereas Jesus, it seems, healed the parts by healing the whole."[10] Clearly, then, spiritual development must be more than an emotional Band-Aid for aching hearts, a painkiller to mask inner hurts, a glib answer to hard questions, or even a security blanket for bad days. Spirituality, rather, is an absolute requirement for a fulfilled life. The prophet's ancient promise is fulfilled in us, "Thou wilt keep him in perfect peace, whose mind is stayed on thee" (Isa. 26:3, KJV).

Spiritual Formation—a Wonderful Gift to Give Yourself

One startling fact overshadows everything else in spiritual development: God stands ready to shape us into Christlikeness at whatever speed we allow. Though not a Christian, the best-selling writer Rabbi Kushner explains the idea: "The purpose of life is not to win but to grow."[11] Thus, spiritual development, when stripped of platitudes and taken beyond good intentions, is more a journey than a destination; running this race is more important than winning.

Spirituality is a ceaseless search for satisfactions that truly matter. Unlike other journeys, there is no place to stop in faith formation. But we won't need to stop because the effort energizes the traveler for the journey. The process gets more satisfying with every exercise. The results are a joyous, lifelong openness to God and a continuous striving for an accurate view of self, the world, and the Father. The sojourner makes commitments to growing goals and cultivates personal mastery.

By definition spiritual formation includes growing, stretching, and maturing—a process that produces positive change. Amazingly, God often shapes us into Christlikeness by using ordinary happenings and routine circumstances. Ideally, this inward journey uses the teachings of Jesus to test our intentions and actions. At the same time, it holds us accountable for all we have received through creation and grace. This gift of interior renovation decreases stress because it cures hopelessness and boredom. Why not be kind to yourself by getting your soul in shape? Why not experience the joy of right living?

- **This gift of spiritual formation connects faith with life.** Spirituality takes us out of the fog into the bright daylight, so that we can pray, "Deep, deep down inside we're hungry, even if we appear to be silly, lazy, or unconcerned at times." Though no secret formula nor fixed time are required, the proven connectors are Scripture, prayer, worship, the sacraments, and Christ's pattern for life. These are the exact resources prophets, apostles, saints, martyrs, and commoners always used to put them in touch with God.
- **This gift of spiritual formation produces positive consequences.** Everyone knows and Scripture confirms that sin and selfishness always issue unwanted paychecks of destructive despair and empty purposelessness—all enormous sources of stress. And death is the long-term wage.

On the other hand, goodness, faith, and righteousness produce good fruit in abundant crops. Love, wisdom, compassion, and closeness to God are common denominators in the truly satisfied life, which has always triumphed in human history. These satisfactions are validated in our own experiences also.

In spiritual development we choose thoughts, behaviors, and relationships that naturally produce positive consequences. That means every requirement of spiritual development actually plants seeds that finally produce an amazing harvest of satisfying consequences to make us happy, complete human beings. What an amazing gift of lasting security, dependable wisdom, and enabling strength.

- **This gift of spiritual formation brings us frighteningly close to God.** It is natural to be timid near God. Like Elijah of old, we are painfully aware that God sees us exactly as we are. He always has and He always will. But spirituality takes us so near Deity that we may feel like Winston Churchill: "I am always ready to learn, although I do not always like being taught."[12]

Nevertheless, this closeness benefits us as it probes

our desires, values, and potential. At the same time, it gives us a sense of belonging like an earthly home—a safe place to be stretched by God's shouts and whispers. Malcolm Muggeridge explains these life-changing encounters with God as a "mysterious exaltation, an awareness that mixed up with the devices and desires of the ego, there are other possibilities and prospects, another destiny whose realization would swallow up time in Eternity, transform flesh to spirit, knowledge into faith and reveal in transcendental terms what our earthly life truly signifies."[13] This relationship with the Father gently yet insistently nudges us to think and behave in ways consistent with our discoveries.

• **This gift of spiritual formation fortifies us.** This inward journey makes us noble enough to face anything and strong enough to endure everything. One year a television reporter quizzed an old, sun-weathered fish camp owner about the critical water shortage when Florida's Gold Coast was threatened because so little rain had fallen into Lake Okeechobee. With little anxiety she replied, "We're survivors around here. We wait awhile, and the Lord sends rain." Soon the clouds dumped torrents of rain on the lake as if in answer to her pluck and prophecy. The drought was over.

In a similar way, spirituality builds survival skills in the soul so that contemporary disciples can wait patiently while God works out His purposes. The results amaze us as we wait awhile and the Lord provides what we need. Then spiritual dryness disappears in a floodtide of grace as the Psalmist's promise is actualized, "He restores my soul" (23:3).

• **This gift of spiritual formation lights fires of hope.** How else can Bob Schewne's passion for godliness be explained? Imprisoned in his own body by Lou Gehrig's disease, Bob was forced to be a spectator at his own slow death. When muscles and nerves would no longer respond to impulses from his brain, he asked to have his Bible placed on a nearby table so that he could turn the pages with his tongue.

Though family and friends considered Bob's situation desperate, he thought of his plight as a bump in the road in preparation for a fast-approaching meeting with God. In getting ready, Bob's spiritual formation activity developed sturdy inner braces that equipped him to deal victoriously with life and with death. To the last day of his life, including weeks on a respirator, he demonstrated indescribable hope for both the present and the future.

Personal experience taught Bob that the Bible summation is true—though the outward person perishes, the inner person is renewed day by day (2 Cor. 4:16). And he taught those around him unforgettable lessons about hope, a charming offspring of spirituality.

- **This gift of spiritual formation helps us cope with troublesome people.** Happy friendships, stable marriages, and joyful parenting are beautiful building blocks for constructing a satisfying life. But we all need help when strange people weary us.

Brother Lawrence, the kitchen saint and the grandfather of practicing the Presence, offered a unique perspective for coping with exasperating people: "When we begin the spiritual life, we should consider and examine to the bottom just what we are. We will find ourselves worthy of all contempt and surely not deserving the name Christian. Knowing all this, we should not be surprised when men trouble, tempt, oppose, and contradict us. We ought, on the contrary, to accept these troubles, temptations, oppositions, and contradictions, and bear them as long as God pleases, knowing they are highly advantageous to us."[14]

Such a view of ourselves and others lowers the stress that comes from strained human relationships. From the Gospels it is clear that Jesus expects us to be nice to His friends, even the strange ones.

- **This gift of spiritual formation overcomes uncertainty about eternity.** Though some think of eternal life as an endless existence starting at death's door, a dying woman gave me a new perspective. At her bedside, I offered the usual words of comfort while she suffered savage pain from multiple amputations and fast-advancing blindness caused by diabetes. "If eternal life is like this," she said, "I don't want it." Shaken by this encounter, I rechecked the Scriptures and began to see that eternal life is a relationship with God that entails infinitely more than endless duration. Eternal life is a relationship where wrongs are righted, injustices are corrected, and pain is healed.

Unlike any other experience, this new life, according to Scripture, starts now and grows better forever. I love the way my four-year-old friend's remark encourages overstressed people: "Heaven is where God puts people back together again."

- **This gift of spiritual formation resources inner inadequacies.** Though a commitment to live out the teachings of Jesus requires more than we can do or be by ourselves, it begins with a will determined to explore the mysteries of the faith-walk. Such a set of the will requires dogged resolve like Old Testament Jacob's wrestling with God: "I will not let you go unless . . ." (Gen. 32:26). However, our limitations show in the sad fact that we sometimes make one choice with our heart and another with our feet. A set will, even when distractions or distortions stress us, means we respond as fully as possible to God's beckoning to solitude, silence, and strength.

But steely human resolve is never enough. Kierkegaard recognized this dependence in his prayer, "Teach me, O God, not to torture myself, not to make a martyr out of myself through stifling reflection, but rather teach me to breathe deeply in faith."[15] To lower stress, a set will must be connected to God's enabling provisions.

Though this spiritual development resourcing sometimes begins dramatically like Paul's Damascus road conversion or Wesley's Aldersgate encounter, it usually continues as a quiet quest, which Jesus described: "Blessed are those who hunger and thirst for righteousness, for they will be filled" (Matt. 5:6). The promise, "they will be filled," makes every effort and longing worthwhile.

Spiritual formation nourishes the whole person including longings, ambiguities, and passions. Consequently, the modern monk's ideal becomes astonishingly real: "If a man is to live he must be all alive, body, mind, heart, and spirit."[16] The resulting inner growth boggles the pilgrim's mind as he sees himself emerging like a butterfly from a fragmented self into an authentic whole person. Surprisingly, the seeker begins observing the Father's likenesses in his own attitudes and actions.

All of this means that when you give yourself the gift of authentic spirituality, it is more than a dull withdrawal from the world or more than a lifelong straining for superhuman religiosity. This gift infuses purpose into life, so that the pursuit of godliness fills the distracting void at the core of human existence. And this gift provides assurance to face life's questions.

Fully considered, spiritual formation is the finest gift of a quality of life you can give yourself. It is God's miraculous provision of inner wellness.

Cotton Fields, Watermelons, and Spiritual Formation

This quest to know God sounds like a story from Ed Husband's childhood in rural Mississippi.

Ed grew up in a black family in the 1930s on a sharecropper's farm where all the children worked of necessity in the cotton harvest. To support the family, his father supplemented his farm income with a laborer's job in town. Consequently, during harvest season before going to his town job, the dad assigned the amount of cotton he wanted each child to pick that day.

Spirituality—Putting Life in Balance / 29

The blazing sun and scarce shade made harvesttime miserable. Day after day the humidity was unbearable. And the more cotton a child picked, the heavier his sack became. The children were pulled constantly between a wish to please their father and a desire to play.

But the father had a refreshing surprise planned for them. Back during planting season, he knew what weather conditions would likely be during harvest; so he buried a few watermelon seeds as he planted cotton. During harvesttime, just when the children were tempted to give up, they discovered a watermelon patch in the middle of the cotton field.

Imagine their delight. Watermelons never tasted so refreshing. Watermelon juice, as it ran down chins and elbows, never felt so cool. As the children feasted, their thirst disappeared and the heat felt more tolerable. Oh, how they appreciated their father's surprising plan for them.

Like the picking chores of the Husband family, the lifelong quest of spiritual development sometimes makes us bone weary. Sometimes we want to quit. But God plants refreshing watermelons in the middle of our spiritual cotton fields.

Each experience along this faith journey whets our appetites for more of God. As we meet Him in our hot, sweaty, frustrating routines, we feast, our hunger disappears, and we are refreshed. As God puts life into balance, we experience "a sense of homecoming, of picking up the threads of a lost life, of responding to a bell that has long been ringing, of taking a place at a table that had long been vacant."[17]

Spirituality integrates mind, body, and soul so that living becomes joyously authentic, internally free, and vibrantly alive. All of this builds an awareness of two important realities—we have enormous control of our lives, and God stands ready to enable us to be and do. As a result, intimacy with God lowers our stress even as it shapes us into

Christlikeness. As our stress decreases, we refocus our energies and establish strategies for growing a quality life.

All these God-given provisions answer John Powell's prayer in us:

> *O Lord, enlighten whatever is dark in me . . .*
> *Strengthen whatever is weak in me;*
> *Mend whatever is broken and heal*
>   *whatever is sick in me.*
> *Strengthen whatever is twisted . . .*
> *Revive whatever joy and peace and life*
>   *that have died in me.*
> *Come, Lord Jesus, be the Companion of my life*
> *And Partner for all eternity.*[18]

> "Christianity is not, as it is sometimes presented and sometimes practiced, an additional burden of observances and obligations but an immense power which bestows significance, and a new lightness upon what we are already doing."
>
> —Teilhard de Chardin

2

SPIRITUALITY— MARKERS FOR THE JOURNEY

The pioneers of spirituality left many tried-and-true markers to point us to God. These giants, so immersed in the realities of Christianity, are more than quaint old-timers with strange-sounding names. Rather their writings direct us to relevance through prayer and contemplation.[1] These trailblazers teach us time-tested spiritual formation principles that apply to our modern situation. These yesteryear saints steer us to meaning in old yet new ways.

Nurturing friendship with the pioneers, however, requires more than examining dusty old books or deciphering crumbling gravestones. Indeed, it takes serious thought to look into their hearts to see what drove them to God. For our own development, we must make the effort because we need to understand the spiritual passions that molded them into Christlikeness. What did they think? What did they know? Why did they write what they did?

To make use of their assistance in untangling our tensions, we must allow them to question our feelings and correct our assumptions. In this life-impacting journey with the masters, we will be surprised to discover that ancient ideas can be very contemporary. Truth, eternally up-to-date, does not always shine with the sheen of originality.

Their markers, still standing like a blazing sun at midnight, grew out of their own struggles. As their faith findings became workable for them, they sought ways to communicate their discoveries to future generations, including ours. Clearly their own understanding of what they found increased in the telling and retelling. And we receive magnificent benefits as they show us the way to wholeness, increase our sense of worth, and lower our levels of stress. Listening to them invigorates our faith even when their word choices and sentence structures sound awkward or outdated.

The pioneers authenticate their instruction for our hectic stress with their overcomings. Rooted in their own faith struggles, their markers inform us that a life cluttered by empty events, fragmented relationships, and debilitating perplexities requires more than a simple formula or even a well-written creedal statement to be healed. Their examples teach that unity at the core of character requires a journey with a Friend, a pilgrimage to the depths, and a commitment to take spiritual resources to the risky frontiers of human existence. Regardless of circumstances, they advise us to seek wholeness in Christ. That is the foundation of spiritual formation.

We need much of what the pioneers had. These masters of the inner life point us to satisfactions that prestige, power, and pleasure can never deliver. To heal our damaged psyches and to relieve our dispirited melancholy, we must hear and heed the pioneers' insistent message: serious spiritual formation makes us whole.

Marker 1—Spirituality Is Strengthened by Struggles

Tragedies and trials come to all, even though no one welcomes pain. In times of despair, life feels like the scriptural summary, "My poor human nature could get no relief—there was trouble at every turn; fighting without, fear within" (2 Cor. 7:5, Goodspeed). Our problem—What can be done when the grind of life creates more questions than human reason can answer?

Though the spiritual masters lived out their answers to this dilemma, they never taught that spirituality is an escape from reality. Struggles for them meant an automatic turning to God, so circumstances never imprisoned their souls. Their sterling examples remind us that secular-saturated living eventually leads to emotional and spiritual crises.

The spiritual masters offer alternatives to our struggles. They agree wholeheartedly with Alice Munro, "Nothing can happen to you that you can't make use of. Even if you're wracked by troubles, and sick and poor and ugly, you've got your soul to carry through life like a treasure on a platter."[2] Though the pioneers never experienced intensities of lives like ours, their insights show us how to overcome our stress.

In the midst of every kind of trouble, these faithful trailblazers show us how to explore the wondrous world within. For them and for us, especially in the midst of crushing problems, life is incomplete until the wide range of God-designed possibilities for wholeness is explored and applied to life. Their guidance agrees with missionary J. Hudson Taylor's prayer: "Don't let pressure push me farther away, but let it draw me closer to You."

Our Source was their strength; He either delivers completely or enables endurance. Either provision was sufficient for them and is adequate for us.

Marker 2—Spirituality Requires Intentional Seeking

Kinship with the giants confirms the fact that serious Christians in every age gave high priority to personal spiritual development. Inge suggests that a composite photo of the pioneers shows "they claim to have had glimpses of a land that is very far off, and they proved they have been there by bringing back perfectly consistent and harmonious reports of it."[3]

These faith formation veterans taught that a yearning for God is an indispensable ingredient of a satisfying life. From experience, they knew that an important way to release the hammerlock of stress, as A. W. Tozer explains, is that these holy people out of the past "mourned for Him, day and night, in season and out, and when they had found Him, the finding was all the sweeter for the long seeking."[4]

One reference point in the literature of spirituality is exceedingly clear—life does not work well for long without a serious quest for God. The wisdom of the ages agrees, and evidence from our era confirms this reality.

Such a wholehearted search requires time, interest, and effort. Jeremiah records the promise, "You will seek me and find me when you seek me with all your heart" (Jer. 29:13). To heal stress problems, ways must be explored to allow God to fill in the details of our lives with himself. Wholeness is the reward "of those who diligently seek Him" (Heb. 11:6, NKJV).

Marker 3—Spirituality Crosses Doctrinal Fences

Across generations, geography, and cultures, our God-hunger links us to a wide variety of religious traditions and encourages us to investigate many sources for insights about the deeper life. An amazing number of common threads turn up in this search. That explains why it is useful to explore all tributaries of spirituality including evangelical piety, medieval mysticism, Catholic monasticism, and the Protestant Reformation. God sometimes flabbergasts us by planting truth in gardens that are unfamiliar to us, though well-known to Him.

Our ancestors in the faith, in spite of differing theological views, nourish the sinew of our souls with rich red meat. Their promise of close friendship with God stretches us to be more than we think we can become. But in an important sense, the masters travel along the trail beside us. Centuries ago, John, the friend of Jesus, delightfully described this life together: "What we have seen and heard we declare to you, so that *you and we together may share in a common life*" (1 John 1:3, NEB, italics added).

These trailblazers from many doctrinal traditions help us understand how spirituality lowers stress and gives meaning to life. As C. S. Lewis insightfully suggests, when we open our hearts to the masters, we enjoy the "clear sea breeze of the centuries."[5] A Christ-shaped life, so highly prized and recommended by the pioneers, draws us to deeper explorations of spiritual growth in company with friends who often sail under a religious flag that is largely foreign to us.

Marker 4—Spirituality Tears Down Artificial Walls

Human beings build Berlin walls to separate life into secular and sacred compartments. Brother Lawrence, a "regular Joe" saint who lived from 1611 to 1692, discovered a satisfying solution to this difficulty. For many years his work was menial kitchen chores at the Carmelite monastery near Paris. Surrounded by smelly garbage and dirty pans, he concluded that life is sacred—all of it.

In his refusal to compartmentalize living into sacred and secular parts, Lawrence tears down walls and opens gates to show us that God is as present in kitchen clatter as in holy Communion quiet. For him, God made the greasy kitchen a place of worship and the Communion table a powerful energy source for daily life. Brother Lawrence's "sacrament of the ordinary" made him see a sacred dimension in every secular event, relationship, and circumstance. So can we. And personal stress decreases when we do.

Marker 5—Spirituality Deals with Self-idolatry

Everyone has a dark side of haughty selfishness, a severely embarrassing cause of stress for themselves and everyone around them. One person described it as a three-ring circus where all the actors and animals compete for attention at the same time with little regard for anyone else. Another called it self-sovereignty, an outlaw against the individual's highest good. Though the reality of the dark side cannot be denied, competition between selfishness and selflessness confuses its victims and causes an inward blush.

The prevalent contemporary life-style of self-fulfillment at any price is this same old distressing sin dressed in new rationalizations. Self-idolatry views submission, self-denial, gentleness, and surrender as groveling signs of weakness.

Strange as it seems, selfish people also often suffer from feelings of inferiority. Though low self-esteem and selfishness appear to be contradictory, they frequently exist together in the dark attic of the same soul. Self-sovereignty, whether its symptoms are pompous assertiveness or attention-gaining expressions of inferior feelings, strangles spiritual health. The problem shows in too much emphasis on I, me, and mine; so the details of life are then measured by their effect on my plans, my dreams, my family, and my security.

This kind of overstress grows out of too much attention to self. Allergic to themselves, these people suffer from an overstrained ego that is in love with itself. Fred Allen offers this description: "The last time I saw him, he was walking down Lover's Lane holding his own hand."[6] As a consequence, these fragmented individuals feel estranged from themselves and others because their inner world is overcrowded by a population of one. In such a state of mind, it becomes obvious that nothing damages faith as much as a neurotic overcare of self. The most crippling hindrance to spiritual development is the erroneous belief that selfishness works. It doesn't.

One description of this stress root can be found in Paul's testimony: "For I have the desire to do what is good, but I cannot carry it out. For what I do is not the good I want to do; no, the evil I do not want to do—this I keep on doing" (Rom. 7:18-19). At least one spiritual formation trailblazer thought such double-mindedness was actually an expression of cowardice and fear; cowardice because we know ourselves too well to run our own show; fear because we do not trust God enough to allow Him to have absolute control. This struggle tenses lots of people, even now.

Augustine describes his emancipation from self-idolatry in his spiritual autobiography. Like many moderns, a civil war raged between competing desires in his inner world. Weary and wary of this conflict, he untied this self-centered, stress-producing knot at the core of his being when he allowed Christ to become "the fulfillment of every aspiration, the answer to every perplexity, the fresh spring which makes all human beings new."[7] A quiet inner truce came as Augustine allowed his Lord into every corner of his life. Being freed of his guilty past and given a hope for the future did wonders for his self-esteem and elevated his relationships with other people. Then his self-evaluation became amazingly accurate.

The lesson for us is that Christ in you produces a wellness in the soul that no self-improvement program can ever provide. A self-image steeped in the perspectives of Christ frees a person from every necessity to put himself down or to exalt himself. The Christmas carol says it so well; when Christ appeared, "the soul felt its worth."

In amazingly up-to-date ways, much of the inner development literature ties self-assessment to authentic spirituality. It teaches that stress growing out of an overemphasis on self is actually eliminated as Christ is allowed to be Master. Then, with Teresa of Avila, "We walk in the truth of who we are."[8]

As a result, the selfless person focuses his whole life on God and others, a sure path to wholeness. Then a valid self-worth emerges that rejects foundationless pride even as it encourages a celebration of talents and abilities. This relationship to the living Christ supplies an authentic self-worth not based on one's job, family, social standing, appearance, education, or intelligence.

Francis Fénelon, who lived in the 17th century, long before modern psychology began, instructs those who are tempted by destructive selfishness or are overly anxious about low self-worth: "Let us compare our life to that of Jesus Christ. Let us remember that He is the master, and that we are the slaves; that He is all-powerful, and that we are only weakness. He lowers himself, and we raise ourselves. . . . To be Christians is to be imitators of Jesus Christ. . . . Let us not pretend to be able to reach this state by our own strength. Everything in us resists it."[9] The good news is that God enables us to overcome this resistance, so that self-centeredness melts like ice in the summer sun as we remember who we are, who He is, and who He wants us to become.

A useful pattern for this Christ mastery is provided by John Wesley, Methodism's founder. In a *Journal* entry of May 25, 1738, he reports: "The moment I awaked, 'Jesus, Master,' was in my heart and in my mouth; and I found all my strength lay in keeping my eye fixed upon Him, and my soul waiting on Him continually."[10] Such delightfully wholehearted attunement to Christ moves spiritual growth from dreary duty to a satisfying life where the Lord is supreme in all things. As a result, the spiritually developing person has good reason to respect his worthy self.

Consider an obvious fact—careful attention to spiritual formation makes us willing to admit insufficiency at crucial moments in our pilgrimage. Then we realize what we had never admitted: There are stronger hands than ours; they are God's hands. There are better thoughts than ours; they are God's thoughts. There are better plans than ours; they are God's plans. And there is greater strength than ours; it is God's enablement combined with His grace.

Consequently, spiritual formation transforms a nobody into a somebody, but this new somebody is freed from haughty struts and obnoxious pride. It is somebody whom God has strengthened to deal with selfish rebellion and develop authentic self-worth so that we can go on, carry on, become, and serve.

Marker 6—Spirituality Gives Meaning to Ordinary Things

Fantasies about fast-lane living cause many strugglers to undervalue the importance of plain folks, everyday events, and things so small as hardly to be noticed. Evelyn Underhill, an example of a spiritual master, deals with this relationship between the routine and the supernatural in her devotional book, *The Spiritual Life*, published early in this century. For the readers in her generation and for us, she explains that faith must be woven into the fabric of human experience: "A spiritual life is simply a life in which all that we do comes from the Center, where we are anchored in God: a life soaked through and through by a sense of His reality and calm, and a self given to the great movement of His will."[11] Authentic devotion to God takes us into the sweaty real world, never out of it. But it is a sacred journey into common life.

In this God-saturated life, the Father uses familiar people and ordinary circumstances as channels for us to give kindness, love, and service. And He uses the same channels on other occasions for us to receive friendship, joy, and correction.

A wee bit of contemplation about this majestic source of simple strength makes Buechner's self-revealing summary relevant: "There is no event so commonplace that God is not present within it, always hiddenly, always leaving room to recognize him or not to recognize him, but all the more fascinatingly because of that, all the more compellingly and hauntingly."[12]

Marker 7—Spirituality Nourishes a Quality Life

Though a thousand voices seduce us with temptation about a quality life, most never make good on their promises. In contrast, spiritual formation always delivers a quality of life as it develops a red-blooded, hands-and-feet kind of faith—this kind of life is vastly superior to a mere high standard of living.

Many markers pointing to a quality life can be found in the compelling writings of Thomas R. Kelly, the Quaker. In *A Testament of Devotion*, published posthumously in 1941, he describes how the inner life nourishes the outer life: "Deep within us all there is an amazing inner sanctuary of the soul, a holy place, a Divine Center, a speaking Voice, to which we may continuously return. Eternity is at our hearts, pressing upon our time-torn lives, warning us with the intimations of an astounding destiny, calling us home unto Itself."[13]

Could homesickness for God be an illuminating way to describe spirituality?

Paul Scherer agrees with this thought when he stirs our hunger for a fulfilled life. Scherer, well loved in an earlier generation as a Lutheran pastor and respected as a New York Union Seminary professor, opens windows of insight when he suggests spirituality helps us escape "from meaningless into meaning, from futility into purpose, from bondage into freedom, from security beset with peril hedged round about by God."[14] His way of viewing life makes us see how underutilized spirituality is in so many lives today.

In another cheer for quality living, Scherer suggests, "There is something thrilling about life when you see it whole—something majestic: the sweat and the blood, the joy and the tragedy."[15] Clearly, this ideal lessens our attraction to trinkets, money, or fame—all crippling sources of stress. Instead, it turns the sight of the soul to what is truly significant.

God's wholehearted kind of living is like an exquisite

art form for Jurgen Moltmann, the contemporary theologian. He suggests that spiritual development should be thought of as constructing a fascinatingly beautiful piece of art in the midst of surrounding ugliness: "Christians are artists and their art is their life. Thus we are artists of life and we are called individually and communally to sharpen our life into an artwork which brings to expression something of the beauty of the divine grace and the freedom of the divine love."[16]

This lovely life of color and form sounds like the apostle Peter's challenging call to meaning, "Be beautiful inside, in your hearts, with the lasting charm of a gentle and quiet spirit which is so precious to God" (1 Pet. 3:4, TLB). Indeed this idea calls to mind a childhood Sunday School song, "Let the beauty of Jesus be seen in me." Emphatically this idea means that a God-fashioned, artful life cannot be allowed to become stress-scarred by apathy, anxiety, or mediocrity.

But how is this quality life to be nourished? Perhaps Thomas Merton, the spiritual giant from the Trappist Monastery near Gethsemane, Ky., can coach us: "The mind that is the prisoner of conventional ideas, and the will that is the captive of its own desire cannot accept the seeds of an unfamiliar truth and a supernatural desire. For how can I receive the seeds of freedom if I am in love with slavery and how can I cherish the desire of God if I am filled with another and an opposite desire?"[17]

His summary is sound. Spirituality calls us to use obedience, faithfulness, and even sacrifice to shatter the status quo. To put it more precisely, this quest for God leads to a balanced life that thrives on relevance and integrity.

Extravagant assistance for developing God's kind of living is available to all. Spiritual formation, though it can never be determined by regulation or code, begins and flourishes with a meaningful relationship with Jesus. Serious sojourners find their hunger to know Christ provides the delightful side effect of a fulfilled life.

Marker 8—Spirituality Overflows in Active Goodness

Mother Teresa of Calcutta enjoys immense satisfaction as she delivers compassionate support to India's dying multitudes. Her care for the destitute in the name of Christ forms the cornerstone of her Society of the Missionaries of Charity founded in 1948 and is the reason she received the Nobel peace prize. To this unassuming nun, spirituality means active goodness—a satisfying way to tie doctrine and servanthood together. For her, spirituality is never passive but always active—something to do as well as feel and believe. Sister Teresa shows us it is the life, not the words, that speak loudest of devotion to God. For her, genuine spirituality starts with contemplation and then rolls up its sleeves in service.

Malcolm Muggeridge asked Sister Teresa in a public interview, "Our fellowmen, or many of them, perhaps including myself, have lost their way. You have found the way. How do you help them find the way?"

Surprising simplicity showed in her response: "By getting them in touch with people, for in the people they will find God."

Muggeridge, like thousands of others, expected a more sophisticated answer. "You mean this road to faith and the road to God is via our fellow human beings?"

Based on her vivid contacts with suffering humanity, she replied, "Because we cannot see Christ, we cannot express our love to Him, but we can always see our neighbors, and we can do to them what if we saw Him we would like to do to Christ."

Then Mother Teresa suggested this moving summary, "In the slums, in the broken bodies, in the children, we see Christ and we touch Him."[18]

Teresa's commitment to India's dying outcasts astounds the world. And though onlookers may suspect her simplicity, they actually find active holiness expressed in heroic deeds on Calcutta's streets. Mother Teresa, driven by an obsession to be like her Lord, is living proof that robust spirituality need not be complex or clever. She is an incredibly impressive example of how faith is married to action in the New Testament.

Genuine wholeness takes root in a life organized around Christ as Dominant Center. Such active service links the inner and outer worlds. It enables people to change the outer world even as it calms their soul, energizes their bodies, and recharges their overextended emotions. Like a recipe for a fine gourmet meal, this sacred journey mixes reason, commitment, faith, and action in just the right proportions to form a life of active goodness.

The Giants Invite Us to the Symphony of Spirituality

Spirituality, to borrow an idea from Underhill, can be compared to a symphony performance where concertgoers are partially deaf. The symphony patrons, because of hearing difficulties, must depend on what others say about the brilliant music. They believe the orchestra plays magnificently because their friends offer such glowing reports and because they hear an occasional note for themselves. So they praise the music without firsthand knowledge.

We are like them. Afflicted by spiritual deafness, most of our information about faith formation comes from others. Though friends share impressive reports, we understand only parts of their message because of impaired hearing. Nevertheless, we believe there is something more wonderful than we dared imagine, because of what the spiritual masters have told us.

In the midst of our impairment, we pray to hear. Then God heals our deafness so that we are able to enjoy the music of the soul for ourselves. And we discover to our absolute surprise that spiritual formation is more magnificent than we dreamed.

The markers left by the pioneers remind us the Father keeps seeking us, all the while we search for Him. This makes us understand the joy of a convert from a D. L. Moody meeting who prayed, "Lord, I thank Thee for going out of Thy way to find me."

Our spiritual ancestors direct us into a God-filled life such described so insightfully by the old Sarum Primer:

> *God be in my head, and in my understanding;*
> *God be in my eyes, and in my looking;*
> *God be in my mouth, and in my speaking;*
> *God be in my heart, and in my thinking;*
> *God be in my end, and at my departing.*

At every milepost of the journey, the markers point us to Jesus, who calls us to translate belief into behavior and faith into a life-style where stress decreases and trust increases.

Spirituality is a life revolutionized by God-nearness.

From our fears and sins release us,
Let us find our rest in Thee.
—Charles Wesley

3

STRESS—DISENCHANTMENT WITH THE SUBSTITUTES

I had a bad day, and to top it off a woman spit in my face because of her dog. I knew I was taking trouble home when I slapped my four-year-old son, Chad, for no reason. I felt I was being swept away. My doctor wrote me a prescription—no sweat." That is how dogcatcher Tony Minor described his overstress to a Fort Lauderdale, Fla., newspaper reporter.

Tony, only 28, requires four daily doses of Valium to keep from falling apart. Unnerved by tension, he said, "I was in very bad shape. I cried for no cause. I couldn't sleep or eat." He has good reason for his tensions. In addition to dealing with stray dogs, he is forced every day to duck obscenities and rocks thrown by angry dog owners. Once an irate canine lover pointed a gun in his face; another tried to run him down with a car. Tony's job has him battered by stress.

Chaos goes with living, like it or not. Along with dogcatchers, nearly everyone is tensed by nerve-racking people, trapped by unresponsive systems, and annoyed by demeaning circumstances. Somewhere, at any given minute, someone is getting sick, being stopped for speeding, receiving bad news from a physician, planning a divorce, or learning that his kid is on drugs. Stress is everywhere.

Stress is exploding through the roof in our society. A crusty old character correctly sized up the situation: "Look around you. Everyone has a problem, is a problem, or lives with a problem." He is right. Too much stuff and too little purpose stress millions. This anxious tension never discriminates because of age, race, sex, vocation, religion, or national origin. And the causes are multiplying.

A working definition for stress is a state of fatigue resulting from too many commitments to causes, relationships, and life-styles that do not produce long-term satisfactions. Like physical pain, these stress symptoms warn us that something needs to be changed. All is not well. Soul, body, or mind—sometimes all three—cry out for something, but who knows what?

Stress—an assembly-line worker in a Detroit auto factory argued with her boss. Sally Fleschman, age 38, regrets her tantrum because she has no husband to help her support her three children. Her stomach churns with unresolved anger. For spite, her foreman transferred her to a job where friendlessness fuels more stress.

Stress—a Florida policeman quit his job because he saw too much in the line of duty. Exposure to pain, frequent shift changes, and court leniency destroyed Parry Watson's ability to function as a law officer. To make ends meet, he took a lower-paying job as a night watchman at a second-rate hotel. Now he fears a heart attack waits around the corner because he feels dizzy and his hands go numb. He blames his old job for his drinking problem.

Stress—an energetic couple, Mike and Melissa, hold responsible, high-paying jobs, but both have unreasonably demanding bosses. To keep up, Mike travels three days each week, and Melissa works 10-hour days. Weekends do not allow enough time to catch up. Mike, though only 38, is frightened by persistent fatigue, chest pains, and stomach discomfort. Melissa, age 36, battles chronic depression that triggers a litany of physical complaints to her family and coworkers. Though Mike and Melissa are terrorized by the treadmill of success, they refuse to admit limitations even to each other.

Stress, the number one malady of Western society, hammers Sally, Parry, Mike, and Melissa. They are not alone in this avalanche of inner fragmentation; the American Academy of Family Physicians estimates that two-thirds of all visits to doctors' offices are prompted by stress-related illnesses. The suspicion that it is getting worse is borne out by our own experience as some deep, undiagnosed force increases blood pressure, triggers depression, and clogs arteries.

Stress grows rapidly in environments where so much energy is spent coping with problems that the purpose for living is forgotten or ignored. That means we are at risk because masses are currently armored in selfish secularism, the emotional sky is frighteningly overcast, the spiritual clouds are threateningly dark, and the daily functioning is toughly tense. Many are disillusioned by jobs. Others, frightened by the loss of spiritual underpinnings, do not know what to call the crisis.

Emotionally battered friends are all around us, and an occasional glance in the mirror brings the problem startlingly close to home.

We are overstressed. The disease is deadly, and it appears to be contagious. This enormous psychic pain demands urgent attention. But how? No one knows what to do. Our attention has been so diverted from lasting values that we have forgotten how to think about what really matters and have nearly lost our way.

Identify the Tangled Substitutes

Some causes of stress remain a mystery, even though researchers keep uncovering additional facts. University of Montreal endocrinologist Dr. Hans Selye, the father of stress research, defines stress as "the rate of wear and tear on the body."[1] He believes the intensity of modern living is the primary cause of tension in most people. Though stress has many causes, the root problem is fueled by the unrelenting obligations of fast-lane living. Convincing clues point to culprits like too much noise, too many opportunities, too many expectations, too little time, too many obligations, too little faith, and too little satisfaction.

Stress is an outgrowth of long-term unfulfillment, aggravated feelings of dissatisfaction, lack of love, and a sense of inadequacy to accomplish ordinary tasks. Tension festers around unhealed emotional pain and grows out of unrealistic expectations of marriages, jobs, or religious experiences. Some people even provoke stress in themselves by refusing to accept who they are.

The pain keeps getting worse because stress never deals with the most pressing human problems: how to give and receive love, where to find satisfaction, and how to find a reason for being.

The killing symptoms are persistent fatigue, intestinal complaints, rapid pulse, insomnia, rising blood pressure, irritability, and lack of concentration.

Like fingerprints, everyone has his own threshold of stress. Psychologist P. W. Buffington, however, suggests recurring patterns based on his research, "There appear to be four central causes of stress: change, unpredictability, lack of control, and conflict."[2] Though few face all these demands on a daily basis, everyone is forced to deal frequently with all four. Regrettably, there is no place to hide from change, unpredictability, lack of control, and conflict. These stress factors are always with us—sometimes like a lashing wind, more often like a trickle of water wearing a stone away.

A thousand minicrises overload our inner circuits, adding up to a bumper crop of stress. Then molehills turn into Mount Everests, so that a child's tantrum, a mother-in-law's visit, or a coworker's gum chewing jangles our nerves and elevates our blood pressure. Surprisingly, the effects keep popping up in physical, emotional, or spiritual symptoms long after the irritations are forgotten.

Many medical experts believe all stress causes some degree of permanent damage, even though tensions accumulate in sly, gradual ways. For this reason, some specialists believe every incident of stress leaves an indelible mark on the body or soul—maybe both. The fallout from anxious tension causes damage in our physical and emotional systems for a long time, perhaps forever.

Efforts to control stress are further complicated by the fact that God has been crowded out of modern life. Herbert J. Freudenberger, M.D., makes an important point: "In a society where we have killed our gods, exorcised our ghosts, separated from our parents, and left our neighborhoods behind, we have little left to cling to."[3] In such a situation, stress should be expected, since spirituality has been deserted along with its buffers to help us deal with frustrating situations, troubling relationships, and aimless activity. For many, their interior life is barren and boring, like a fake birthday present with colorful wrappings and dazzling bows still in place.

Examine the Exhausting Feelings

Studies over the last 20 years show that stress triggers body chemistry changes, so tense situations ignite several physical systems to get us ready for fight or flight. After calling stress an internal congestion, Norman Cousins explains: "Our experiences come at us in such profusion and from so many different directions that they are never really sorted out, much less absorbed. The result is clutter and confusion. We gorge the senses and starve the sensitivities."[4] Apparently stress, significantly more than a single out-of-kilter emotion, is a tangled web of thoughts, feelings, and actions that gang up to threaten our equilibrium.

As a result, weary exhaustion—an accurate portrayal of cluttered living—does not improve after 10 hours of sleep or a long vacation. Nouwen paints a powerfully realistic picture of this tiredness in the soul, which so many experience in this era of perpetual vagueness: "Fatigue—*physical*, because of lack of sleep; *mental*, because of lack of motivation; and *spiritual*, because of lack of inspiration—takes over and leads to neutral resignation, growing irritation, or even eroding depression."[5] Many admit, in candid moments, to being tired like that, even though they slept well last night or have not overworked for years. Perhaps the most grueling strain of all comes from the fact that we are detached from what really matters.

Feeling out of control is another graphic way to explain how stress affects us. Pressured persons easily identify with Arthur M. Schlesinger's summary of Robert Kennedy's Vietnam trauma: "An indefinable sense of depression hung over him as if he felt cornered by circumstances and did not know how to break out."[6] It is doubtful that Kennedy ever got Southeast Asia out of his mind or body. Nearly everyone has at least one similar source of stress. These complicating anxieties vex beach bums, construction workers, corporation presidents, supermoms, grocery clerks, medical interns, waiters, and us.

No one is exempt. The human body, originally designed to clear unplowed fields and fight furious beasts, is now tensed by tight budgets, rebellious teenagers, unresponsive bureaucracies, computer errors, undependable air travel, and gridlock traffic jams. One overstressed woman wrote in her journal: "Whatever chemicals my body was dumping into my bloodstream were so potent that I could feel my face flush, my heart race, and my muscles tense. Everything was racing inside." On an occasional basis, such arousal may cripple; but when it happens continually, it means slow, agonizing self-destruction, emotional illness, or even death. Blame our galloping tempo, spiritually bankrupt life-style, and foolhardy chase of worthless stuff.

High stress lathers us up, but modern life offers no way to work it off or lay it down. Everyone knows it is unacceptable to flee from demanding responsibilities and against the law to strangle obnoxious strangers. So we stew in self-generated stress secretions.

Admittedly we are frightened when our heart races, perspiration increases, muscles tense, and a sudden burst of adrenaline rushes into our bloodstream. These ill-defined perplexities are accelerating so quickly that one devotional master warns, "The whole mechanism of modern life is geared for a flight from God and from the spirit into the world of neurosis."[7]

Compute the Mind-boggling Cost

Though no one knows the bottom line, stress steals millions each year from employees and employers, even as it negatively impacts national and world economies. Though it is impossible to calculate the total cost, the National Institute of Health estimated as early as 1978 that stress costs American industry $10 billion annually in absenteeism, medical expenses, and lost productivity.[8] The price tag multiplies every year. Costs explode even more as overstressed workers prove eligibility for workmen's compensation due to job-related stress illness. Some experts believe the annual cost equals the national debt.

Only a few decades ago, stress situations were considered regrettable, and that ended the matter. In slower, more quiet times the duration of tension was intermittent, so people could bounce back between crises. The situation is vastly different now—our entire society is awash in stress-related problems. Today lethal warnings in books, magazines, newspapers, and on TV and radio feed our stress awareness. And we talk about it more, much more. Everyone wants this grim murderer stopped before he kills again, but who knows how?

Other costs must be considered. More expensive than

dollars and cents, there is the intangible inner pain that contributes to emotional distress and spiritual bankruptcy. And there is more. Medical authorities suspect stress to be a major contributing factor to cancer, lung ailments, cirrhosis, accidental injuries, and coronary disease. New discoveries linking the mind to the immune system suggest that the way we think affects us right down to our cells.

Other well-documented suspicions warn that prolonged stress heightens existing illness, sets the stage for new diseases, and may even encourage viruses and infections. Dr. Jeremiah A. Barondess of Cornell University Medical College summarizes the research: "Stress today is not only one of the common factors in symptomatic ills that brings people to their physicians; it may also be an important factor in predisposing and sustaining organic disease."[9]

Another nonfinancial though demanding human cost comes from bland boredom that destroys people by inches. Individuals are discontent, not because they have nothing to do, but because they wonder if what they do matters. Others are miserably unfulfilled by purposeless activity; deep down they know mere motion does not provide meaning.

All this leads to a significant fact—there must be sufficient tension to keep life interesting but not enough to cause damage. Dr. Donald A. Tubesing, author of *Kicking Your Stress Habit,* advises that like a violin string "you need enough stress to make music but not so much that it snaps."[10]

All of this makes us conclude that overstress apparently originates in two contradictory ways—from meaningless boredom or overscheduled living. Its not-so-secret weapons are outer distractions and inner dissatisfactions.

The whole price, if every cost could be computed, would be unbelievably high in both financial and human terms. This skyrocketing monetary total reaches into billions each year. At the same time, the intangible costs rob nearly everyone of some degree of peace; Dr. Regis A. DeSilva underscores the seriousness when he says tension often pulls the "psychological trigger for cardiac arrest."[11]

Avoid Overreacting to Life

Plainly, stress is more choice than chance. To be stressed causes confused thinking, and to be confused in one's thinking causes stress. No one knows whether stress comes from wrong thinking or stress causes wrong thinking. The theologian Reinhold Niebuhr shines light on the issue when he says Augustine was a man who "saw very clearly that it was not the mind which governed the self, but the self which governed the mind."[12] We do know that thought significantly affects the intensity and duration of stress.

Apparently the damage stress causes does not result only from outside conditions, events, or people, but from an individual's response to situations. Only three options exist in stress-caused experiences: (1) compliance; (2) change of circumstances; or (3) change of response. For situations that can be changed, energy, creativity, and commitment should be invested to make things better, especially those problems caused by our own behavior. But stress is also intensified by too much focus on problems in the environment, weaknesses of other people, and circumstances over which we have no control; we allow outside forces to control too much of our lives.

All these stress problems are compounded by the fact that thoughts and feelings can be deceptively tricky. Edmund Spenser once summarized, "It is the mind that maketh good or ill, that maketh wretched or happy, rich or poor."[13] Distorted thinking causes lots of stress. Thoughts can be misshapen or false.

Though jobs, schools, friends, and bills get blamed for tensions, it is the individual's reaction to these issues that causes most stress. The real causes are within the individual—we all have some control over the choices that arouse our inner grump. Unnerving as it seems, much of the stress poisons flowing into our inner world started with self-induced inaccurate thoughts, unrealistic expectations, or unreasonable reactions.

Perhaps that explains why the same event or relationship either toughens or traumatizes us, depending on our responses. With every mistaken reaction to life, a kind of overheated thinking consumes us, so we feel beset by too many problems, too many duties, and too many options. We need to admit to ourselves that we are to blame for stress when we believe pure hokum.

Happily, the exact opposite can be true. We can think our way out of stress. That is the precise reason why illogical dimensions of stress must be recognized and abandoned. Consequently, one crucial stress management factor is the willingness to challenge our own obsessive thoughts, inaccurate perceptions, and disagreeable notions. Sometimes a simple readjustment in our thoughts drastically affects the circumstance or changes the way it looks to us.

By working on ourselves, the conditions can be improved enough to make the situation tolerable or even satisfying. Conversely, by allowing the circumstance to remain the way it is, we curse the darkness, allow outside forces to imprison our thoughts, and give unfavorable events power to control us.

The needed formula: accept what we cannot change and change ourselves at the same time. An example is a troubled marriage; one partner can become more loving and accepting. A drastic improvement in the marriage may result. But if not, the one who improves his or her own acceptance of the situation experiences growth because of the change within.

We all make choices like that about stress, even though they are unaware of it. A couple chooses whether a new baby opens doors to exciting bonding or traps them with demanding routines. A retiree determines whether the slower pace offers exhilarating freedom or life-threatening disappointment. A vacationer decides whether time away from a job provides renewal of mind and body or frustrating boredom. Everyone walks this thin line of choice between fulfillment and anxiety.

While exploring ways to teach his patients how to control tension, Robert S. Eliot, M.D., developed the term *hot reactor*. Eliot, as an overstressed cardiac victim himself with a short-fused Type A personality, explains in his book *Is It Worth Dying For?* that many tense people habitually overreact to life. He goes on to observe, "Some people experience alarm and vigilance so strongly that when they are under stress their bodies produce large amounts of stress chemicals, which in turn causes significant changes in the cardiovascular system, including remarkable rises in blood pressure."[14] These high-voltage types spend $1,000 worth of energy on a penny-sized problem, though they do not know why. Typically, hot reactors attack every part of life with such rigorous intensity that they give high priority to everything, making catastrophes out of small stuff.

Though this hot reaction pattern is difficult to break, a healthy view of life makes us realize how disappointing events or obnoxious people sometimes save us from bad decisions and additional stress. This long-range view, much to our relief, helps us accept the fact that all potentially stressful relationships or circumstances may not be bad in an ultimate sense.

To retrain skewed thinking about stress requires that a distinction be made between stressors and stress. Stressors, the causes of stress, begin with a demand to adapt to life that pushes the individual to react. However, it is the feelings, the thoughts, or the words that finally cause stress. Consequently, a decision, however weak, has to be made by the potential victim before stressors are able to activate stress. The significance one attaches to the circumstance determines the level of stress that will be experienced. This means the health of our inner world is determined by the sum total of our thoughts. The Bible states the issue succinctly: "As [a man] thinketh in his heart, so is he" (Prov. 23:7, KJV).

Potential stressors surround us everywhere; the list is endless and complicated. For example, emotional stressors trigger tension about bills, love, and war. Family stressors fuel worry about single parenting, empty nests, aging parents, blended households, or two-parent careers. Even seemingly quiet environments contain potential stressors to keep us constantly keyed up. The solution, then, revolves around the question, how can we keep stressors from triggering toxic stress and making us into emotional or spiritual wrecks? Clearly, a more satisfying life demands that stressors be managed.

Research shows that stress decreases dramatically when we gain control over stressors by changing the way we react to irritating people, nagging incidents, or daily drudgery. The literature offers a variety of formulas to help. Surprisingly, many of these formulas restate time-tested principles that the Bible has taught for 3,000 years. Consequently, tension can be greatly lowered as spiritual development encourages self-understanding, accurate thinking, and Christ-centered living.

Convincing evidence makes us conclude that we can reason our way out of stress just as we thought our way into it. To do that, an individual must cultivate an attitude that says, "I will not use emotional H-bombs for little things. I resist using high levels of energy to deal with petty irritations caused by money, possessions, or position."

Spiritual development helps with this process because it profoundly affects the way we think, feel, and react; it enables a person to see life accurately. That means spirituality offers us a readily available stress remedy as it helps us form a realistic view of our stressors. We must think better to feel better.

Maybe It's Time to Try God

Because a large portion of stress comes from ignoring the roots of faith, many can easily identify with my college friend's bumper sticker, "Since I gave up hope, I can laugh." Clearly, the brassy, insecure laugh sounds like Thomas Merton's description of our disenchantment: "We are caught in the ambiguities of a colossal sense of failure at the moment of phenomenal success. We have everything we ever claimed to have wanted, and yet we are more dissatisfied than we have ever been."[15]

A telling sentence in a *Fort Lauderdale Sun-Sentinel* editorial on substance abuse has wider application: "When nothing else is working, maybe it's time to try God."[16] Could it be that rattled nerves and addled thoughts are pushing moderns to trade stress-producing success, competition, hoarding, and greed for God, love, faith, and becoming?

This inner wellness—God's gift of wholeness—feeds on the worship of God and exposes us to the contagious teachings of Jesus, so we gladly forsake all lesser pursuits to follow our Lord to the heights and depths. Pastor Lloyd J. Ogilvie suggests a spiritually focused stress management system: "All we need to do is to ask God to take charge of our minds, infuse our nervous systems with His Spirit, and control our body responses."[17]

To make the soul well, spirituality remedies rush, froth, hurry, spin, shallowness, and emptiness. Then the disenchanting substitutes are replaced with the reality of God himself.

The ultimate solution for stress is to live life God's way.

> "We can keep ourselves so busy, fill our lives with so many diversions, stuff our heads with so much knowledge, involve ourselves with so many people and cover so much ground that we never have time to probe the fearful and wonderful world within."
> —John W. Gardner

4

HUNGER FOR THE HOLY

"Is there something more?" That is the haunting question a young Jewish law professor asked the class as he concluded a brilliant guest lecture at Vanderbilt Divinity School.

His self-revelation shocked the students: "I am a yuppie, tenured professor at Vandy. My life sounds like the American dream. I have a beautiful wife and two bright kids. I live in a big house and own two expensive cars. I am not happy, even though I have everything any mother ever wanted for her son. I thought you religion guys might have some answers. Is there something more?"

The professor's yearning personifies the fact that stress increases when spiritual growth does not keep up with intellectual or vocational development. Evidently the Vandy students felt the same emptiness, because not one attempted to answer the professor's question.

And thousands outside universities are also famished for significance. This hunger for the holy is described by Judith C. Lechman as an "awful yawning emptiness created by God's absence."[1] Though stress is multifaceted, it is often deeply rooted in spiritual incompleteness.

Moral Erosion Intensifies Our Hunger for the Holy

Moral erosion surrounds us as redefined values zoom the moral Richter scale through the roof. Dissatisfactions are increasing. Violence mocks the Golden Rule. Rip-offs by corporation raiders and petty thieves have replaced business honesty. Children and women are abused or abandoned. Many young adults, raised without moral guidance, lack interior resources to face even minor crises. Marriage covenants are casually broken by divorce and infidelity. Meanwhile the elderly have had their confidence shaken by a decreasing quality of longer life.

In such a topsy-turvy world, the voices of so-called brilliant individuals insist they do not believe in God; their laughable logic insists they have outgrown a need for Him. Such pseudosophistication shows they have been duped by high-sounding nonsense that only increases their stress. Others keep looking for newer sensations because they are bored by ordinary routines.

At the same time, a confusing inner tug-of-war pulls this generation between self-assertion and self-surrender. Many seem determined to disprove the abiding fact that the world is built on moral foundations. Indeed, these attempts, like arguing against gravity, only illustrate the necessity for spiritual principles to guide life.

Stress snowballs during periods of moral erosion. Examples include Karl Marx, Sigmund Freud, and their disciples, who indelibly imprinted their views on modern society. Though both Marx and Freud died mired in despair by their own conclusions, the aftershock and side effects of some of their theories continue to create tensions for millions to this day. Even a superficial comparison of the Ten Commandments with our current moral mess highlights the fermenting frustration people feel.

Moral cancer cripples and eventually kills individuals with overstress. Erosion of values debilitates groups and nations. When we candidly face our situation, we are forced to agree with Dag Hammarskjöld: "You cannot play with the animal in you without becoming wholly animal, play with falsehood without forfeiting your right to truth, play with cruelty without losing your sensitivity of mind. He who wants to keep his garden tidy does not reserve a plot for weeds."[2]

In this morally confused society dizzied by crumbling absolutes and fatigued by incredible pace, fed-up people cry out, "Where does all of this lead?" The obvious answer is, "Nowhere." Nevertheless, we keep ourselves dazzled with incessant hurry down dead-end streets to nothingness. It should be no surprise; this situation is a natural outgrowth of too little faith and too much activity. The problem is not in the world, but inside us.

High-tech Confusion Intensifies Our Hunger for the Holy

Technology is a mixed blessing. Computers have revolutionized contemporary society fully as much as the printing press, electricity, or railroads reshaped earlier periods of history. Modern weapons threaten everyone. Defense spending has nearly bankrupted the world. The media, especially TV, has become a vendor of smut and gloom.

Birth control has changed sexual values, medicine, family sizes, and school populations. Jet travel has made the world a global village and opened new business markets around the world. Smaller technological advances like supermarket scanners, microwave ovens, fax machines, phone-answering devices, and automatic bank tellers have changed the way we live and think. And now VCRs have shifted the entertainment habits of millions, so videos can be rented from grocery stores.

These changes cannot be undone, nor should they be. Nobody wants to make war on progress. The dilemma— technology improves modern living at the same time it alarmingly increases stress for millions.

Psychology Professor Stanley Aronowitz believes "stress has become the black lung disease of the technical class."[3] He is precisely correct in the example of Mark Tighe, a 31-year-old software programmer for Digital Equipment Corporation in Colorado Springs. Tighe's story is an amazing intrigue between technology and stress. During the very early hours of a September morning, Tighe left his semirural Woodmoor home for a 15-minute drive to his work place. Evidently he arrived about 3:30 A.M., when he logged in on his computer and composed a suicide note. Mark taped the sheet to the wall after the printer typed his message. At 3:59 A.M., before shooting himself, he opened fire on a $200,000 VAX computer system in what appeared to be a final statement of what computers had done to him. Security guards discovered him dead near his computer keyboard about 6:30. Later that morning police found his girlfriend's body when they forced their way into Tighe's rustic house. Apparently she had been murdered by a .45 that lay on the floor near the waterbed.[4]

Though investigating officers may never know all the facts in the Tighe case, this apparent suicide and murder illustrate the intensity of stress caused by technology. After allowing for emotional distress and severe fatigue, serious questions must be asked of a technical society that pushes people to the edge with corporate mergers, scientific wizardry, and high vocational mobility. Mark's interest in life ran out because he drove himself too hard for too long in a stress-producing jungle.

Clearly high tech tenses those involved in its design, manufacture, and distribution, but technophobia also infects those who are forced to use it. Now that computers and other electronic devices have moved into most businesses and homes, there are those who fear the equipment is too complicated, workers who feel undertrained, and employees who have been automated out of a job. Such high-tech changes put everyone on pins and needles.

Albert Einstein was right: "Technological progress is like an ax in the hands of a pathological criminal."

Good Life Seductions Intensify Our Hunger for the Holy

"Seduced by the good life" is the way one highly placed industrial mogul describes our ferocious race to get ahead. Beyond befuddling pressures like the expected need to sell oneself to a job, less-obvious deceivers lurk around every corner. It is worsened by the fact that we have too little time, too many choices, too few values, too many demands, and too few lasting commitments. But there is a growing suspicion somewhere deep in the human spirit that preoccupations with food, power, sex, busyness, and money have made the so-called good life lopsided, so we feel underwhelmed by integrity, peace, and love.

Desmond Wilson, the actor, discussed contradictions of the good life with Michael Dougan of the *San Francisco Examiner:* "I bought the great American dream. I attained wealth and success and the world was an empty, desolate place for me." He continued, "My children didn't bring me any satisfaction. And my wife didn't bring me joy. I didn't know how to love people; I tolerated them." Well remembered for his role as Lamont in the TV comedy "Sanford and Son," Wilson went on to be Oscar in "The New Odd Couple." Raised in Harlem, he joked about his childhood, "My parents were in the iron and steel business—my mother ironed and my father stole." Though Wilson grew up the hard way, at the height of his acting career he owned a fleet of luxury cars, a 27-room Bel Air mansion, and everything that goes with such affluence. Still he was dissatisfied. His possessions owned him.[5] His conclusion keeps repeating itself—fast-lane living costs too much and pays too little.

A senior from a prestigious Eastern university reached the same judgment through a different series of events. After joining the Peace Corps, but before leaving for his assignment, a Fortune 500 corporation representative offered him a fabulous, high-paying position. The recruiter, using what he considered his most convincing argument, told the graduate, "You will become rich if you abandon the Peace Corps and work for us." The student, energized by a desire for meaning, answered with a compelling question, "What's the big deal about having lots of money?"

Anyone who chases money must answer that question for himself.

Greed, a near universal vice, fools us into strange ways of behaving. George McDonald exposes this tricky snare: "If it be *things* that slay you, what matter whether things you have, or things you have not?"[6] All this insatiable grasping wrecks relationships, stresses the heart, and sears the soul. As a result the good life easily turns into a hellish merry-go-round that never stops because greed always grasps for more.

Chasing the good life also mocks high achievers. Though big breaks and best salaries are promised to the most talented, unusual ability sometimes causes petty jealousy in the workplace. Then mediocre employees resent the procedures, so threatened coworkers and tyrannical supervisors find sadistic gratification in keeping gifted people in dead-end vocational slots. Sadly, destructive results follow for everyone: talented workers feel like overly controlled pawns, the enterprise is weakened, and decision makers die a little inside when they think about their actions.

Fast-lane living, with the satisfaction that it never delivers, adds to the confusion. Epictetus, the ancient Greek, once observed correctly, "Man is disturbed not by things but by his ideas about things."[7] Indeed, stuff, securities, and status con us.

However, an additional life-changing issue must be factored into this misdirected quest for fast-lane living.

Wherever a good life leads, however alluring or interesting, it is incomplete without Christ. No one has it all without Him. A person is always a pauper if he has everything but Christ. Therefore, those who desire the truly good life must include Jesus; no one else on the playing field faintly compares with Him. To have everything but Christ is to live in the most frightening kind of poverty, but to have nothing but Christ is to possess everything that matters.

Ceaseless Motion Intensifies Our Hunger for the Holy

Our daily activities overload our stress circuits. Some days it seems as if the whole world is running a marathon race to who knows where. In an amazingly bewildering book, *In One Day—The Things Americans Do in One Day,* Tom Parker details the whirlwind activism of contemporary people who are nearly overwhelmed by an avalanche of unfulfilling tasks. Each day Americans eat 815 billion calories of food, 200 billion more than we need; spend $700 million for entertainment and recreation; drink 1.2 million gallons of hard liquor with a bar tab of $64 million, 1.5 million gallons of wine, 15.7 million gallons of beer and ale (or 28 million six-packs); pay $40 million for prostitution; give $165 million for charity; pick up the $2.5 million tab for car washes; and plunk down $40 million for auto repairs. The incredible list goes on—every day we buy 190,000 wristwatches, 120,000 radios, 17,000 videocassette recorders, 4 million books, 250,000 neckties, 325 pounds of cocaine, have 500 coronary bypass operations, and spend $125,000 on merchandise and tours associated with the memory of Elvis Presley.[8] No wonder millions feel strained to the breaking point and beyond.

Though reading the list makes one tired, consider the vast energy needed to coordinate the schedules and the hungry budgets required to accomplish these things. And what about the tidal wave of worthless results? Our consumer society is infected with affluenza, "an array of psychological maladies, such as isolation, suspicion, boredom, guilt, and lack of motivation, engendered by wealth."[9] And for empty people, this ceaseless activity complicates the problem because it turns each new day into a repetition of a hundred unsatisfying yesterdays. Perpetual motion never drives the dread away.

An incredibly powerful antidote for these stress sources shines through this monologue with God: "Lead me, even though it be against my will, into Thy way . . . Through doubt, through faith, through bliss, through stark dismay, through sunshine, wind or snow, or fog, or shower. Draw me to Thee who is my only way."[10]

To avoid a half-lived life, divine resources must be allowed to relieve our breathlessness and strife in the soul. A genuinely fulfilled life is not possible without God.

Meaningless Religion Intensifies Our Hunger for the Holy

Masses believe religion has lost its soul. Even though they may be vaguely aware that a crisis of faith surrounds them, many miss the message of Christianity because they have heard only shrill marginal voices. Many on the street have no concept of solid faith because they have been exposed to such a narrow slice of the real thing. Some have met Christians who undermine the cause of Christ because they are frightful boors. Religious show biz turns others off.

Regrettably these spiritually illiterate people, being faith lazy, seldom seek out answers for themselves at church, in private conversations, or in books. Consequently, ideas like spirituality, piety, and meditation elicit ignorant or negative reactions from them. Fénelon describes their lack of information: "They only know what religion extracts, without knowing what it offers."[11]

And another foreboding issue must be added to this equation. An alarmingly high percentage of religious leaders have nothing to offer overstressed seekers because they themselves are too busy chasing counterfeit relevance, professional status, or personal gain. It is regrettable but true that lay and clergy leaders on many levels of church life display a sad spectacle of self-serving priorities planned to advance their own authority, control, or careers.

These impoverished functionaries work in a self-imposed environment that one writer calls a "reservation of the spirit—a safety zone set aside for religious conversations that do not affect thought, conduct, or culture." Of course, their fuzzy thinking and high-sounding verbiage mean precisely nothing. By forsaking their own inner moorings, these so-called religious leaders have trivialized faith so that they have nothing to offer secularists. Yet thousands mistakenly think these leaders represent the real thing.

The need for authentic spirituality deepens even more when one considers the fossilization of some churches. One contemporary pastor reports, "Most congregations of professing Christians today are saturated with a kind of dead goodness, an ethical respectability rooted in the flesh rather than in the illuminating and enlivening control of the Holy Spirit."[12] This summary underscores an anemic, tragic situation. The church, when weakened to flesh and bones, can offer only puny pabulum to the most stressed generation in human history.

But there may be reason for hope because severe stress sometimes awakens latent spiritual sensitivity and potential. To overstressed people the need for faith becomes more obvious when life caves in and they are forced to deal with grim realities. Then, even practicing atheists feel a necessity to think second thoughts about faithless secularism when cancer invades their bodies, when sexual disease kills friends, when economic greed threatens their living standards, or when grown children join cults in search of a reason for living.

Was ambiguity ever more glaring? So much has changed that it is difficult to comprehend the meaning of all this transition. But the world must be getting ready for something. New hunger for freedom sends shouting protestors into the streets. Pornography and television violence fires folks to protest to unresponsive civic leaders and to TV station owners. Teenage pregnancies, divorces, and abortions rip the fabric of family life. Scientific discoveries and medical delivery systems scramble long-accepted assumptions. Even though a secular mind-set has a stranglehold on the media and public debate, people are afraid when life turns threatening. The Gospel writer records Christ's amazingly accurate description of the present situation: "Men will faint from terror, apprehensive of what is coming on the world" (Luke 21:26).

Perhaps the day has finally dawned to let some fresh air in and pay thoughtful attention to Albert Day's idea: "The power of a life where Christ is exalted would arrest and subdue those who are bored to tears by our thin version of Christianity and wholly uninterested in mere churchmanship."[13]

There may be hope; this epidemic of powerless religion when mixed with acute stress could drive people to God in desperation.

An Unsatisfied Self Intensifies Our Hunger for the Holy

Think of the search for a safe place to stand and for a remedy for our interior illness. John T. Benson described this plight as an unsatisfied, mysterious me, an uncommitted, unfulfilled self at the core of human experience. Though abstractions and aggravations may blur the unsatisfied self, it shows in our ceaseless search for a person to become. This vague vacancy of the spirit, an overactive mind or body connected to an undernourished soul, is much more than a biological, psychological, or emotional force at work in us. This inward void requires more than we can think with our minds or feel with our senses.

Unfortunately, many try to satisfy this mysterious emptiness in self-defeating, silly ways. Nearly everyone can think of a ridiculously laughable example: A 75-year-old man, after striking up a partnership with a questionable geologist, goes off in search of oil where it has never before been found. Or a multiple divorcée, tormented with scalding memories of four marriages, actively seeks another husband while feeling like a tramp in embarrassing moral exile. The middle-aged executive, though he has amassed a safe-deposit box full of securities and a garage full of gadgets, tells his psychiatrist, "I feel unfilled." This mysterious self, if left unattended, leads to a wasted life.

But this unsatisfied self, when directed toward God, encourages the first steps toward faith, potential, and creativity. Fulfillment always starts with God. If directed, this hunger for the holy can take the unsatisfied, mysterious me to God's highest resources for growing a satisfying life. Spiritual formation leads to more meaning than one can imagine. It provides in us the answer to Paul's prayer, "I pray that your inward eyes may be illumined, so that you may know what is the hope to which he calls you" (Eph. 1:18, NEB).

Stress—Does Life Make Sense Without God?

Many thoughtful people believe too much was lost when biblical teachings were kicked out of contemporary life. The observation of my 85-year-old friend has much value, "I like up-to-date ways, but I still need old-fashioned faith." Though spirituality appears old-fashioned to sophisticated cynics, it is timeless in the sense that it takes us back to the ancient, radical teachings of Moses, Jesus, and Paul. Though spirituality is one of the few cures we have for stress, it is more than enough.

However, pressing questions still persist in some minds: Is spirituality real? Is it a mere pensive religious binge? How can spirituality be attained? Though these concerns deserve a thoughtful answer, a prior question must be considered first: Does life make sense without faith?

I found the answer in a conversation with a little Jamaican grandmother. When I questioned her about how long she had followed the Savior, she answered, "Since I got sense." She is right. Can anyone deny that life without God is an absurd joke?

Back to previous questions. All around us clues show that the inner life is as real as the physical world. God keeps showing up everywhere. And though unseen realities seem nebulous when compared to the material world, our hunger for the holy is much too real to be dismissed as mere myth. That is why doubters have trouble explaining hope at a new grave, denying intimacy with Deity at worship, or doubting the satisfaction of giving a cup of cold water in the name of Jesus.

The alternative must also be considered. Accumulation has disappointed so many people that they desperately desire something more than newer cars, bigger houses, larger paychecks, or fair-weather friends can provide. Millions, though it may not be directly expressed, are apparently bone weary of activity without purpose, brilliance without faith, money without values, sophistication without substance, and stuff without satisfaction. However, they are not interested in religion that offers nothing more than nostalgic childhood warm fuzzies to soften the harsh edges of pressing pain. They want authentic reality. They want to know God in substantial, fulfilling ways. They hunger for the holy.

Spirituality—an Underutilized Interior Health Resource

Though spiritual development is sometimes accused of being superfluous or melancholic, its main concerns are authenticity and meaning. Faith formation gives us a Christ-focused perspective on life, which helps us understand our challenges, question our difficulties, and evaluate our achievements.

As all of life is opened to God, spirituality provides a

Center for organizing thoughts, feelings, and values. It enables us to find significance we lost in living, wisdom we lost in knowledge, and truth we lost in information.[14] Spirituality, this underutilized remedy for relieving stress, develops noble strengths in us and offers wholeness no matter how intense and difficult our tensions seem to be.

Restoring miracle cures for overtense living come singing across 13 centuries in St. Patrick's hymn:

> *I arise today through*
> *God's strength to pilot me:*
> *God's might to uphold me,*
> *God's wisdom to guide me,*
> *God's eye to look before me,*
> *God's ear to hear me,*
> *God's word to speak for me,*
> *God's hand to guard me.*[15]

When these resources are put to use, spirituality cures old cynicism, heals inner civil wars, remedies enslaving doubts, and provides recuperation from exhausting pursuits of lesser gods.

This Christ-centered life satisfies our hunger for the holy. Then all is well, and the Psalmist's testimony becomes our own: "I shall not be in want . . . He restores my soul" (Ps. 23:1, 3).

Remedies for Stress

> *"Religious faith is not a storm cellar to which men and women can flee for refuge from the storms of life. It is, instead, an inner spiritual strength that enables them to face those storms with hope and serenity. Religious faith has the miraculous power to lift ordinary human beings to greatness in seasons of stress."*
> —Sen. Sam J. Ervin, Jr.

5

CULTIVATE THE CENTER

Steeple-high expectations danced in the young minister's head as he moved into his first church. His dreams were soon shattered, however, by a small, disheartened congregation shackled by inadequate facilities, shrinking attendance, and limited funds. His meager salary made it necessary for him to work outside his parish as a substitute high school instructor, where he taught nearly every subject, including cooking, auto shop, and physical education. Raging stress, like an uncontrollable fever, infected him so that he felt strained beyond human limits.

Then trivial problems compounded his misery. He felt so shackled by his growing anxieties that he secretly longed for a quiet heart attack; then his parishioners might provide the emotional support he so desperately needed. At the same time, he feared a nervous collapse would require a costly hospitalization. To resign would create discouragement for his struggling flock and an additional sense of failure for him. Consequently, the young pastor wrestled through months of sleepless nights until he felt utterly spent with nothing more to give. His ambiguities mounted as his exhaustion deepened because he could not see even a shadow of an acceptable solution.

This struggle is intensely familiar because I was that pastor.

Life lost its savor as I felt pulled in all directions, often incapable of prayer. Hopelessness poisoned my soul during that predicament. In the midst of such chaotic powerlessness, I found my link to the Center when a caring friend loaned me *A Testament of Devotion*.

In that book Thomas Kelly explains how life is simplified when it is organized around Christ as the Hub of everything else. He describes a compass in the inner depths of a human being that is magnetically drawn to Jesus just as an external compass is attracted to the north pole. The resulting centering offers a unified way of looking at the world, clarifies a person's self-understanding, and provides a sense of direction for life.

As Center, Christ completes our incompleteness at the same time as He satisfies our starvation for significance. Centering on Jesus, as a way to make sense of life, provides inner orderliness and produces energy to resource all dimensions of life. In this age of bewildering disconnectedness, such a wholehearted attentiveness to God provides "a handle on everything—a focus around which to organize all else."[1] Nothing is too immense or too tiny to keep God from being life's Center. Centering gives meaning to the human journey.

Centering Normalizes Life

For some, the centering idea conjures up complicated mental images too otherworldly to be practical and too mysterious to discuss. Such assumptions, however, are grossly inaccurate because everyone needs such a single focus to organize all thought and behavior. Centering normalizes life by allowing Christ into the corners and crannies, so that a holistic perspective shows up in thoughts, monitors conversations, questions attitudes, and evaluates achievements. At the same time, centering avoids sterile, sublime otherworldliness that confuses the man on the street and has no concrete meaning for the person in the church.

In this Christ-saturated life, competition between the secular and spiritual become irrelevant as Jesus is allowed to be what He really is—Alpha, Omega, and everything in between. Christ, as the organizing Center of life, is like gravity to the universe, a computer chip to a computer, the North Star to a navigator, radar to a pilot, A to a musician, a root to a plant, oxygen to human life, a frame of reference to a philosopher, a chief executive officer (CEO) to a business, a gearbox to a transmission, a linchpin to an axle, and mission control to an astronaut.

Even as software controls the function of a computer, a Christ-centered life sorts out the differences between the essential and peripheral, the ultimate and the temporary, the eternal and the passing.

Based on the valid biblical assumption that the outside always reflects what is on the inside, the writers on spirituality use graphic terms to describe how this inner Center actually impacts life. C. S. Lewis calls Him the secret Master of Ceremonies. Thomas R. Kelly uses unifying designations for Christ, like the Mastering Life Within, the Holy Whisper, Divine Abyss, Holy Presence, and Divine Taproot. E. Stanley Jones calls Jesus the Near Side of God. Richard J. Foster expands our centering concepts with terms like Fountainhead, Reference Point, Spring, and Heavenly Monitor who affects all of life. To be "in Christ," the apostle Paul's phrase, is to choose to be a love slave—the only satisfying tyranny ever experienced by human beings. After a lifetime of thinking, writing, preaching, and observing, one devotional master called Jesus the Divine All.

While living in an environment where nearly everything influences us away from Christlikeness, this centered life shapes the way we think, live, and respond to others. This Near Side of God provides enablement for developing healthy homes. This Holy Whisper shows us how to heal broken relationships. This Source enables us to overcome destructive habits. This Inner Presence replaces loneliness with His nearness. This Holy Center deals with our fear of the future by promising to be actively present in every tomorrow. At the core of our being, this Mastering Life demands a willingness to yield control so that Christ can be President, Managing Director, and Treasurer.

The most obvious benefit of integrated living is intimacy with Christ, who tunes human experience to faith. This intimacy guides, motivates, and resources the details of our daily existence. Therefore, centering makes us more human and more alert to God.

Though spirituality never keeps fog from rolling into life, it stabilizes the inner world so that we can more easily tolerate threatening winds and crashing seas. Christ, as the Hub of human activity and the Magnet of our surrender, deals with unanswered mysteries, joyous discoveries, and frustrated confusion; all are blended by Him into useful purpose. In centering, Christ invades our smiles and tears, our picnics and funerals, our work and play. This "in Him" life takes Christ into corporate boardrooms, company cafeterias, factory assembly lines, computer seminars, family kitchens, school classrooms, and believers' bedrooms.

Centering Shifts Focus from Self to Christ

Centering, an intentional shift from self-directedness to Christ-directedness, begins with a determined resolve to give careful attention to the inner issues of being, motives, and intentions and less concern to appearances, images, and good impressions. This makes Jesus the Significant Point for thought, speech, and action, so that life can function as it was originally intended by the Creator. Centering redirects life by harmonizing everything around Jesus, the Central Calm. Then stress goes down because "all things hold together" in Him (Col. 1:17).

The possibilities are amazingly attractive, simply because all other centers fail finally. Certain things are obvious in our contemporary situation, even though we struggle not to see them—a life centered on spouse, children, job, pleasure, privilege, hero, friend, or self ultimately disappoints us. Fortunes are lost in a moment from one bad decision. Careers are destroyed in a day due to deteriorating economic conditions or a boss's whim. Education and skills can be outdated in a year. Family relationships may be fractured overnight with death, divorce, or desertion. Expand the list in any direction, and it is easy to see that all lesser centers are undeniably temporary.

In contrast, a wholehearted focus on Christ supplies an enduring cornerstone for a satisfying life. Then when sophisticated distractions whirl around us like an emotional cement mixer, this intentional development of the inner life is fed with the Psalmist's affirmation, "I seek you with all my heart" (119:10). Much to our surprise, even the first faltering attempt unblinds our eyes, unstops our ears, and opens our minds to the real sources of fulfillment.

Centering furnishes a real reason for living, so that we "move and have our being" in Him (Acts 17:28). Essentially, this intentional part of centering requires us to surrender the controlling interest of everything to Christ—all authority must be yielded without reservation to Him. This means we imitate Jesus' pattern of submitting our self-centered will to God. Then, Christ is forever in charge without a hint of resistance from us, so He shapes the totality of life. That saves lots of agony and encourages authentic commitments to issues that matter.

Centering Heals Conflicts

Conflicting commitments, however small, stir whirlwind tornadoes in the soul. The results wreck the quality of life. Fulton J. Sheen describes a victim of these inner storms: "While keeping very active on the outside, he is passive and inert on the inside, because he rarely enters into his own heart."[2] In such a muddled state of mind, folks ask, Is life more than a series of problems from the cradle to the grave? and What do I do with my unresolved riddles?

These perplexities between the inner and outer worlds sound like Charlie Brown at a disappointing baseball game. When Lucy misses the ball, she apologizes, "Sorry, Manager, but my body doesn't seem to want to do what my brain tells it to do." Charlie replies, "I understand. My body and my brain haven't spoken to each other in years." That is an accurate portrayal of uncentered living; interior fragmentation feels like a continuous feud between body, soul, and brain.

Holy Scripture describes uncentered people as double-minded. From sad personal experience, everyone knows about this Vietnam war in the soul where every interest of the untamed self insists on having its own way. Like a stormy stockholders' meeting without a chairman, the business self, family self, parental self, and childish self make divisive, simultaneous demands. Such inner anarchy makes the victim cry like a spoiled two-year-old and fight like a combat soldier.

These contradictory feelings are so bewildering that one part of the inner world is active and another reflective; one part noble and the other cowardly; one side aggressive and the other lazy. One side withdraws in defeat while the other wants all-out war. Like Jekyll and Hyde, a portion of the inner world rebels against authority, yet another flatters those in high places. This division in the inner world cripples faith, harms futures, and destroys significant relationships.

This soul fragmentation causes us to spend enormous spiritual or emotional energy on nonessentials—a massive cause of stress. Uncentered living takes a person down a thousand dead-end streets. To be more exact, an uncentered individual lives in baffling vagueness that eats into the fabric of his soul. Consequently, a bridge to the Center is desperately needed, even though it seems difficult to find.

Kelly shows the way: "We have hints that there is a way of life vastly richer and deeper than all this hurried existence, a life of unhurried serenity, peace, and power." He continues, "Each one of us can live a life of amazing power, peace and serenity, of integration and confidence and simplified multiplicity on one condition—that is, *if we really want to.*"[3] Such possibilities sound too good to be true and too good not to be true. Our overstressed minds question whether peace, serenity, integration, confidence, and simplification are even possible. But if the Center is allowed to coordinate all facets of who we are and what we long to become, these results are abundantly possible. Everyone needs this Fixed Point as the Anchor for their existence.

Centering Exposes Homemade Idols

Human beings have tried since creation to understand their reason for being. The search continues. Deep down we have been disappointed so often by fake remedies and false ideals that we are tempted to believe Shakespeare's sad summary that life is "a tale / Told by an idiot, full of sound and fury, / Signifying nothing." But in more sane moments, we know there must be a way to satisfy the deep need for purpose we feel. There is.

However, it is important to consider that genuine centering takes more than commitment to empty causes or plodding through meaningless religious exercises that have been tried many times, in many places. The ancients, like us, sought answers from their homemade gods. The Greeks and Romans went to ridiculous extremes by believing that a whole family of gods directed their lives, so they assigned war, wind, agriculture, and even sex to various deities. And they invented additional gods as new needs arose. Striking similarities exist among Norsemen, Aztec, and American Indian religions. But worshipers in every culture experience annoying frustrations and increased stress when their make-believe gods show themselves to be deaf and powerless.

Modern people have the same letdown feeling when stuff, style, and security control their lives but provide no meaning. Though no marble shrines memorialize our make-believe deities, enormous energy and money are wasted on questionable values and consumed on passing religious fads. Often contemporary folk seek fulfillment at all the wrong places by assuming that a different relationship or a new gadget will satisfy their inner longings. But it never happens.

And we really know why. Blinking yellow lights in our inner world caution us against the insanity of expanding the accumulation of unneeded belongings and unsatisfying relationships. Centering corrects these confusions by refocusing our attention and interests on lasting values and enduring issues.

Centering Encourages Intimacy with Christ

A fragmented life creates muddled uncertainties, a situation complicated by the moral shortsightedness of this era. These baffling feelings sound like my son's insightful comment during high school years, "Dad, do you know how many voices I hear in my head?" All uncentered persons, from their own past or present, have experienced this emotional feeling.

Dag Hammarskjöld, the spiritually-minded Swedish diplomat who served as United Nations secretary-general from 1953 until his death in a plane crash over Africa in 1961, explains the beginning and results of his own centering: "I don't know Who—or What—put the question. I don't know when it was put. I don't even remember answering. But at some moment I did answer 'Yes' to Someone—or Something—and from that hour I was certain that existence is meaningful and that, therefore, my life, in self-surrender, had a goal."[4] Centering abundantly resourced Hammarskjöld's service at his influential pinnacle as a world statesman. The Christ-centered life offers identical enablement to truck drivers, neurosurgeons, ditchdiggers, designers, and us.

Once this centered life is experienced, no one wants to return to the old fragmented way. A simple meeting with Christ puts Him in our heart forever. Then, like the experience of the prodigal in the Bible, the Father is always with us, calling us home wherever we go, whatever we do, and whatever we become.

This God-closeness shapes us in an ultimate sense, even when complexities stress us or simplicity tempts us to be suspicious of the strengths offered in spiritual formation. With Philip we pray, "Lord, show us the Father and *that will be enough*" (John 14:8, italics added). And He is. A fulfilling serenity flourishes in the inner world of all who live in such intimate contact with Jesus Christ.

Nevertheless, Christ never moves to the center of anyone's inner world without that person's wholehearted invitation.

Thomas R. Kelly offers a series of questions to help us find our way into the centered life: "Ask yourself: Am I down in the flaming center of God? Have I come into the deeps, where the soul meets with God and knows His love and power? Have I discovered God as a living Immediacy, a sweet Presence, and a stirring, life-renovating Power within me?"[5] Though Christ kindles every stirring toward godliness, He always waits for our invitation as an important prerequisite for centering.

It is assuring, however, to know that Jesus is patient even when we are slow or confused. Thomas, the doubting disciple, is an example; at a despairing moment he did not know what to believe as he dealt with the heavy weight of an unknown future. Jesus listened kindly to Thomas' questions, though our Lord usually displayed little patience with armchair agnostics. Thomas, trying to cope with frightening fragmentation in his inner world, questioned, "Lord, we don't know where you are going, so how can we know the way?" In a surprising response, Jesus caused Thomas to doubt his doubts when He positioned himself as the Center of all human existence: "I am the way and the truth and the life" (John 14:5-6). As a result, Thomas experienced new hope.

The living Christ did not merely point Thomas to a way, but He claimed to be the Way—without Him there is an unbridgeable distance between God and man; the Truth —without Him there is colossal ignorance of God; and the Life—without Him there can be no genuinely quality living. The songwriter underlined the significance of this Holy Center for Thomas and for all who follow after him:

> *He is the Way, without Him there's no going;*
> *He is the Truth, without Him there's no knowing;*
> *He is the Life, now and eternally.**

Integrated living, Christ's answer to today's maddening complexity, begins when He is allowed into the details of the human journey. Mother Teresa of Calcutta makes the concept workable: "Christ is the Way to be walked, the Truth to be told, and the Life to be lived."[6] The living Lord unifies every aspect of our being around himself. That is centered living at its best.

George Herbert's prayer, even though it comes from the 17th century, takes us to the Center in an up-to-date way:

> *Come, my Way, my Truth, my Life;*
> *Such a Way as gives us breath:*
> *Such a Truth as ends all strife:*
> *Such a Life as killeth death.*[7]

---

*"The Way, the Truth, the Life," by Anita Grund Koch. © 1967 Heart-Warming Music Co. Used by permission of Benson Music Group Inc.

Centering offers alternatives to absurdity, security, ambiguity, success, and failure. Companionship with the Way, the Truth, and the Life unravels uncertainties. Centering nourishes the inner life from the Holy Spring in a minute-by-minute refreshment that allows Christ to bring fulfillment into our work, walk, study, or play. Then when circumstances baffle us, centering allows us to ask God, Why is this happening? Centering helps answer our question, What can I learn from this experience? In the centered life, everything makes more sense because of Him.

Consequently, the extravagant promise of Scripture becomes real to us: "Seek ye first the kingdom of God, and his righteousness; and *all these things shall be added unto you*" (Matt. 6:33, KJV, italics added). Then it is possible to sing the Psalmist's song, "He shall be like a tree planted by the rivers of water, that bringeth forth his fruit in his season; his leaf also shall not wither; and *whatsoever he doeth shall prosper*" (1:3, KJV, italics added). In the centered life we pray with John as he prayed for Gaius, "I wish above all things that thou mayest prosper and be in health, *even as thy soul prospereth*" (3 John 2, KJV, italics added).

From these passages, we see that a centered life crackles with adventuresome, unexpected promise. This integrating resource "sets the dumb to singing and causes cripples to sprint through a host of cynics."[8] To center in Christ is not to stifle or limit life but to enable and empower it.

Helps for Centering

One critic objected to Voltaire's writings by insisting nothing could be as simple as the French satirist made it. Similar roadblocks to spiritual development are created by many writers and teachers. Admittedly, centering is not as easy as it first appears, but neither is it as difficult as some try to make it. The main roadblock is giving up our habits of self-sovereignty.

Centering promises to provide a radical new way of living. Let us begin.

1. Think Small. Many continuously seek religious highs, thinking they function best when something big is going on. Perhaps this explains extravagant financial support for television preachers and may be the reason vicarious excitement is experienced when missionaries tell snake stories. But it is frighteningly easy to sleep through a more quiet nearby spiritual revolution. There are exceptions, of course, but bigger is not always better, and louder is not always more true. There is much good to be found in routine days, even when they seem ho-hum.

So for inner health, seek deliverance from the spectacular and explore the ordinary. Elijah learned from his Mount Carmel victory and later from despair under the juniper tree that God surprises us by bypassing earthquakes to speak in a quiet voice. Vance Havner, the Southern Baptist evangelist, correctly preached, "Woe unto us if we are so deafened by the whirlwind that we cannot hear the whisper."[9] Spirituality need not be sensational to be supernatural.

2. Make a Faith Statement with Your Life. Thomas R. Kelly taught that a centered life is a heaven-directed life.[10] If he is right, many of us need to redirect our thoughts and actions. Though we seldom think about it, our way of life advertises what we believe. Our choices either give credibility to our values or question them. What we believe affects our work, worship, and play; and the way we work, worship, and play publicizes our values to the world.

It may be useful to think of the truly centered life as a nonverbal front-page headline that points people to God. My life is most attractive to others when I am spiritually strong enough to deal with my strains.

To center life in Christ means we welcome His promptings to test our attitudes and activities against scriptural teaching; then religious abstractions become flesh-and-blood issues. This Center of Control gives us an inner yardstick to help us make sense of feelings, emotions, and sensations.

3. Listen Carefully to People and Events. Though God can teach us what He wants us to know in a thousand ways, we must cultivate receptivity. Unexpected treasures await us as we probe Scripture and quiz devotional writers with the question, What is God saying to me here?

Everyday happenings can be observed and questioned too. Amazing wisdom sometimes originates from conversations with aged adults. An unknown writer opens another source when he mused, "We get better acquainted with ourselves by listening to little children." And sunrises and harvest moons direct our thoughts to the Father's magnificent provisions.

Listening to events and circumstances can include that which is close by and simple. Ordinary things like a bee on a flower, an ant on the ground, or a snowflake on a glove can take us to the Center. Jesus used common sparrows to question despair and everyday lilies to discredit worry (Matt. 6:25-32). Catastrophic happenings can do it too, like an auto crash, bankruptcy, a health crisis, or the death of a loved one.

Be ready to receive God's messages from all sources, both ordinary and unusual. Keep your heart open to admire maple trees, smell roses, or hear robins.

4. Practice the Presence. Though large numbers of Christians have vague notions about Brother Lawrence's idea of "practicing the presence of God," few do it. Frank Laubach recounts his own experience: "This concentration upon God is strenuous, but everything else has ceased to be so. I think more clearly, I forget less frequently. Things which I did with a strain before, I now do easily and with less effort."[11]

Practicing the presence immunizes us against preoccupation. It tunes us to God; consequently we see reasons for praise in all of life. Start practicing the presence by asking God's approval on letters you write, phone calls you make, books you read, and television programs you watch. The possibilities are limitless.

5. Allow God to Test Your Truthfulness. In many relationships there exists a kind of clever, deceptive speech, somewhat close to fact, which by flattery, pretense, or tone misleads like a lie. Sad but true, it is possible to become so skilled at doublespeak that others think we believe one thing when we actually believe something quite different. In this age of hype, exaggeration, technical jargon, and image building, it is frighteningly easy to subtly abuse truth. But in the centered life all communication must be screened for God's approval to avoid a hypocritical piety and to be sure it is truly true.

There is another kind of mesmerizing speech, one-thousandth of a centimeter from a lie, which uses high-sounding vocabulary to impress the gullible and uninformed. Its seductive goal is to make the speaker appear impressive, pious, and even brilliant.

But when Christ is allowed to check our speech and silence, we will be more like what we want people to think we are. Ask yourself questions about your truthfulness: *(a)* Do I use words or phrases with double meanings? *(b)* Do I say exactly what I mean? *(c)* Do I pretend to know when I don't? *(d)* Do I use high-sounding words to conceal my ignorance? *(e)* Do I put family, friends, or business associates off with a wait-and-see reply that I never intend to act upon? *(f)* Do I overstate the truth because I want to appear to have a positive mental attitude or create a favorable impression of myself or my work? *(g)* Do I use "I forgot" as a socially acceptable lie to keep from fulfilling a commitment or dealing with some uncomfortable accountability?

Judge the color, intent, and details of your speech to see if it warrants Christ's approval. The goal is to please Him rather than to impress others or fool ourselves. Then there will be no need to fear Albert E. Day's warning, "At the end of a single day, the proud, arrogant thing that set out in the morning with banners flying will come home at night like a bedraggled army beaten and disgraced."[12]

6. Be Satisfied with Enough. Nearly everyone spends too much energy on our society's entrenched notions about money, security, and ownership. These days, no one is completely free from money stress—either we do not have enough, we want more, or we are trying to keep what we have. To deepen our relationships with the Center, we must view secularism's pull through Thomas R. Kelly's perspective, "God plucks the world out of our hearts, loosening the chains of attachment. And He hurls the world into our hearts, where we and He together carry it in infinitely tender love."[13]

Since the Father has assured us that the smallest creatures are objects of His care, why not turn your security hang-ups to Him. Enough is enough, and greed is a seductive liar.

7. Open Your Dark Side to Christ. Apply Francis de Sales' advice to your dark side: "Come now, my soul, we can do better."[14] Too often we do not admit our dark side even to ourselves. These days, making a favorable impression or building an image has such high priority that it never occurs to some strugglers to face this problem. God, however, is never surprised by our destructive side nor our desire to hide it, because He knows us so well.

Though we sometimes have difficulty recognizing this problem in ourselves, clues increase as we focus everything around Him. Embarrassing illustrations show up in disloyalty to people we love, disappointment over unanswered prayer, anger at God for unexplainable events, temptation to greed, or selfish dominance over people at work or home. Glenn Clark offers a solution: "Supposing there is some old root—greed, lust, jealousy or hate—that seems so ingrained in your very bones, in your very nervous system, in your very blood, that there is no way of getting out. Then, lean back and let Christ work the miracle."[15]

8. Resist Distractions. It is difficult to hear God when silence has been exorcised out of our world and households sound like urbanized war zones. Our noisy world vibrates with screaming jets, barking dogs, jangling phones, crying babies, beeping computers, plus blaring televisions, radios, VCRs, and compact disc players.

In order to hear God more effectively, one must intentionally cultivate the capacity to listen. One capable Catholic nun, when invited to be a speaker at a great university, responded with a postcard: "Dear, I am trying to be still." This centered life requires purposeful silence if we are to hear God accurately. We have a built-in need to be still and know that He is God (Ps. 46:10).

One way to quiet distractions is to think intently about a name or attribute of Jesus; try Savior, Lord, Emmanuel, or Redeemer. Useful attributes include love, mercy, peace, or hope. Another centering technique is to recall and dwell on the meaning of Bible words like faith, patience, meekness, or righteousness.

Some single-minded pilgrims overcome distractions by listening more carefully to Scripture. The following examples of Scripture will lower tension and distractions: "It is more blessed to give than to receive" (Acts 20:35, KJV); "Ye shall know the truth, and the truth shall make you free" (John 8:32, KJV); "You are worth more than many sparrows" (Matt. 10:31); "For to me to live is Christ, and to die is gain" (Phil. 1:21, KJV); "Who shall separate us from the love of Christ?" (Rom. 8:35, KJV); "The effectual fervent prayer of a righteous man availeth much" (James 5:16, KJV).

Silence improves concentration, an important component of centering. Should you experience mental drifting, tell yourself, "I'll think about that later; right now, I'm centering on Christ." Then return to the name, attribute, or Bible promise you were using to center on Him.

9. Relive Jesus' Life in Your World. Nothing cultivates the centered life as much as a continuing remembrance of Jesus. Think often about His goodness, mercy, truth, love, and grace. Try to see the world through His eyes and respond as He would. What would He do in your home or office? What does He think about your primary relationships? What would He say about a trying situation in your experience? How would He spend your paycheck?

This effort to think and act Christian can be greatly enhanced by following Paul's directive: "Finally, brethren, whatever things are true, whatever things are noble, whatever things are just, whatever things are pure, whatever things are lovely, whatever things are of good report, if there is any virtue and if there is anything praiseworthy—*meditate on these things*. The things which you learned and received and heard and saw in me, *these do,* and the God of peace will be with you" (Phil. 4:8-9, NKJV, italics added).

10. Share Spiritual Discoveries and Dreams. Spirituality flourishes in relationships; your journey of faith will always be strengthened when you share your aspirations with a trustworthy, spiritually mature friend. Then, too, there is nothing so powerful you can do for another as to give him opportunity to be involved in your quest for Christlikeness. As a result, the inner flame is fanned by like-minded people and sustained through the flat times by caring friends.

You accomplish three significant things when you discuss your personal spiritual goals with someone: *(a)* The fact someone knows your dreams keeps you from sliding into the never-never land of pious fog and good intentions; *(b)* an informed fellow struggler inquires about your progress and cheers you on; and *(c)* you generate encouragement to help others in their own spiritual formation. Sharing discoveries, resources, and skills satisfies a personal need and develops a sense of partnership in a friend's development. The relationship energizes both persons and forms a cornerstone for long-term, happy association with a soul friend.

> "Music is a fair and glorious gift of God . . . Singers are never sorrowful, but are merry, and smile through their troubles in song. Music makes people kinder, gentler, more staid and reasonable . . . The devil flees before the sounds of music almost as much as before the Word of God."
> —Martin Luther

6

SING YOUR STRESS AWAY

Music soaks strength into the soul. God inspires composers to join texts with melodies, and He creates sopranos, altos, tenors, and basses to help us sing our faith songs. This gift expanded even more when the Father enabled craftsmen to build instruments like guitars, tubas, violins, and drums. Vitality that comes through music, like an artesian well, can never be stilled or used up.

A while ago, Bill and Gloria Gaither's music transformed Florida's Lakeland Civic Auditorium into a unique setting for worship. They forged an inspirational connection between musicians and concertgoers by connecting singable tunes to unforgettable words. That evening, Christ-exalting music brought God and the people together.

The Gaithers, a legend in their own time, were assisted by talented vocalists, gifted guitarists, vigorous drummers, and capable keyboard artists skilled on exotic instruments like electronic synthesizers. But something beyond their platform performance affected me—it was an unforgettable encounter with God that came as I shared the evening with friends whom I have loved for more than two decades. Though the evening was extraordinary by any standard, it was the spiritual vitality of the music and the joyous fellowship of old friends that transformed the concert into a memorable meeting with God. That experience produced an awesome memory that sings resilience into my soul even now.

In a short time, the Gaithers' singing made faith real, even as it chased glum weariness and woebegone stress away. "Hold on, my child, joy comes in the morning" drove doubt away. Three words, "He touched me," brought past miraculous meetings with Christ to mind.

An eight-year-old sang, from the top of her voice "I am a promise, I am a possibility." Her solo made listeners cherish children, and hope for future generations was reborn in a moment. Then Larnelle Harris moved quietly on stage to sing the Grammy winner, "I've Just Seen Jesus." His song caused many to relive Mary's empty tomb discovery and reminded us that the Resurrection stands as the undisputed centerpiece of the Christian faith.

About midpoint in the concert, the Gaither Trio sang, "Yesterday's gone and tomorrow may never come; / We have this moment today." Instantly, memories went back to earlier experiences of faith. That song enabled listeners to treasure the present, freed them from the tyranny of the past, and released them to anticipate brighter tomorrows. Though old songs never bring back old times, the message in the music indelibly imprinted our hearts forever.

Music possesses an amazing power to grip us in incredible ways—from bread breaking to lovemaking. Singing stimulates patriotism, motivates worship, and strengthens family ties. Clock radios wake us with peppy tunes and close our days with sleepy-time lyrics. Easy listening music soothes us in dental offices, on jet airplanes, and in waiting rooms. Recorded melodies accompany our first cry in hospital delivery rooms, and church organs peel out our last funeral hymns. Music pursues us all the days of our lives.

Songs so compellingly impact us that it is almost impossible to sing and cry at the same time. Who can complain while thinking about a great hymn? And who can carry a grudge while whistling a happy tune? But anyone can sing and pray at the same time. Thinking gratitude and singing "All Hail the Power of Jesus' Name" go well together. New strength comes during testing times as we hum "How Great Thou Art." Mental tunes like "My Faith Looks Up to Thee" and "A Charge to Keep I Have" revive our drooping spirits, even when circumstances seem to justify cynical pessimism. One short phrase from a beloved hymn puts iron in our will and courage in our soul. Singing makes faith contagious.

Music leaps across miles and years to take us to sacred places on wings of memory. Familiar tunes remind us of the times a hymn wandered through our yesterdays. Because of this inspiring capacity to impact our inner world, hymns are much more than note-by-note arrangements of pitch, frequency, and amplification. The songs of faith help us recall forgotten blessings, heal raw nerves of heartbreak, and carry us back to cherished encounters with God. The music of spirituality inoculates us against much of the damage stress can cause.

Hymns Supply Marching Songs for Pilgrims

God wants us to use music to turn sighing into singing as we travel through uncharted territory. The potential verve of a song shines through Paul Goodman's prayer: "Teach me a travel song, Master, to march along."[1]

Once God used a song to heal my fragmented inner world as I walked along the Atlantic Ocean. To me the rolling tide sounded like a melancholic background for my sadness, and my despairing mood made me feel victimized. My sense of fairness had been battered by lies and exaggerated half-truths spoken by fellow believers.

Even though my wounds were painfully raw, I tried singing. I admit the tune sounded off-key, the words were garbled, and the volume was embarrassingly loud. As I started singing, a charming elderly couple out for their morning walk surprised me and received an earful of my boisterous song. Though my singing polluted their morning, it impacted me in a way I never want to forget.

As I sought answers from God, a line from a childhood hymn shamed my self-pity. Inner renewal started when I began singing Johnson Oatman, Jr.'s, "Count your many blessings, name them one by one, / And it will surprise you what the Lord hath done." The lyrics revolutionized my outlook, so that I was amazed at how the Father was working in my life. The hymn affirmed my confidence that God ultimately controls everything.

My oceanside experience illustrates the fact that musical praise creates a climate where spirituality flourishes and stress melts away. Worries vanish when we sing "God Will Take Care of You." Chilling despair thaws when we sing with fellow worshipers,

> *O God, our Help in ages past,*
> *Our Hope for years to come,*
> *Our Shelter from the stormy blast,*
> *And our eternal Home!*
> —ISAAC WATTS

Streaks of dawn begin to light the darkest valleys when we sing "He Leadeth Me."

How good of God to provide reassuring hymns in our distress. Negative moods vanish when the singing starts, and faith deepens when a gospel song blends scriptural teaching with personal experience. The music of faith crystallizes courage and stimulates spiritual adventure.

Songs of Faith Lower Tensions

Disciples have known for centuries that singing and spirituality belong together like love and marriage or a horse and carriage. Mental health specialists, however, have recently rediscovered music as useful therapy for persons whose inner world reels between lost faith and false idols. The use of music has become so common in treatment that universities now offer music courses to train psychiatric professionals. This renewed use of music underscores what believers have known for generations—singing faith songs soothes tensions and heals damaged emotions.

Resources for inner health flow to us from Horatio Spafford's hymn written shortly after his four daughters died at sea. He wrote while his grief was fresh, "Whatever my lot, Thou hast taught me to say, / 'It is well, it is well with my soul.'" His song had at least two miraculous results—it sang strength into his own soul and ignited hope for thousands from his time until now.

Francis of Assisi, during the weary closing days of his life, found strength to cope with near blindness and intense pain by writing and singing,

> *All creatures of our God and King,*
> *Lift up your voice and with us sing . . .*
> *Ye who long pain and sorrow bear,*
> *Praise God and on Him cast your care!*
> *O praise Him, O praise Him!*

Now hundreds of years later the blessing continues because no one can sing Francis' hymn without being buoyed by the composer's confidence in God.

Though Joseph Scriven intended "What a Friend We Have in Jesus" to comfort his distressed mother, the lyrics show he was no stranger to personal heartbreak. His bride-to-be drowned on the night before their wedding, and when he became engaged a second time, his fiancée died from a dreadful disease. To this day, the encouragement Scriven intended for his mother revives in every human being who sings his hymn along lonely trails, in isolated nursing homes, beside hospital beds, in mission chapels, or in cosmopolitan city churches.

During times of terrible testings, hymn writers, singers, and weary pilgrims seem to team up in a conspiracy against stress by singing songs of faith. Their singing either made their stress bearable or eliminated it altogether. In gracious provision, God has preserved their songs to do the same for us. Consequently, when broken dreams nag us with bewildering perplexity, it is a good time to sing,

> *Jesus! the name that charms our fears,*
> *That bids our sorrows cease;*
> *'Tis music in the sinner's ears;*
> *'Tis life, and health, and peace.*
> —CHARLES WESLEY

While singing stress away, it is easy to understand why Martin Luther believed we could sing even when our problems make it difficult to pray.

Stress, sometimes defined as being fed up with things as they are, always fuels pessimism. At those times, it is easy to allow hopelessness to almost overwhelm us. But self-pity disappears when we sing,

> *Strength for today and bright hope for tomorrow—*
> *Blessings all mine, with ten thousand beside!*
> *Great is Thy faithfulness! Great is Thy faithfulness!*
> *Morning by morning new mercies I see;*
> *All I have needed Thy hand hath provided.*
> *Great is Thy faithfulness, Lord, unto me!**
> —THOMAS O. CHISHOLM

Such a song causes us to see life as it is—a colorful tapestry of blessing and burden, victory and valley, privilege and pain.

Ethel Waters knew how to share a song's vitality. She shouted before her solo at a Graham crusade meeting, "Who needs social security when we have heavenly security!" Then she sang these simple lines with incredible energy:

---

*Copyright © 1923. Renewed 1951 by Hope Publishing Co., Carol Stream, IL 60188. All rights reserved. Used by permission.

I sing because I'm happy,
I sing because I'm free,
For His eye is on the sparrow,
And I know He watches me.
—Mrs. C. D. Martin

Her assuring song lifted crushing loads from everyone within hearing distance. And in my soul I sang too.

God intends for the music of faith to shape us into the image of His dear Son. Each new trial offers another opportunity to sing stress away and makes it possible for us to generate hope with our singing. Henry Van Dyke's hymn is utterly true: "Ever singing, march we onward, / Victors in the midst of strife."

The Sounds of Music Appear Often in Scripture

In an age when cynicism enslaves the human family, Anderson School of Theology Dean James Earl Massey urges us to put our ear close to sacred Scripture to hear the Lord's songs: "Music must gather up our ideas, feelings, wishes and dreams; it must stir our anticipation and it must prod us to place ourselves affirmatively at the very disposal of what the music means."[2] That is what God did when He wove music into the fiber of the Bible so that we can more accurately hear His message.

Imagine how invincible the people of Israel felt while singing, "The Lord is my strength and my song; he has become my salvation" (Exod. 15:2). That rousing refrain, sung after crossing the dry seabed on the day God saved them from the Egyptians, jogged their pessimistic memories and drove stress-producing doubt away. Their singing shamed their sulking and forced them to remember His faithfulness.

The Psalms, the oldest hymns of Christian heritage, show how singing stimulates spirituality even as it lowers stress. In staccato language, Ps. 28:6-7 supplies several reasons for thanksgiving: "Praise be to the Lord, for he has heard my cry for mercy. The Lord is my strength and my shield; . . . my heart leaps for joy and I will give thanks to him in song." The Psalmist broke into spontaneous singing when he inventoried the unfailing grace of God. The Old Testament people knew from their long history that music quickens adoration even as it drives tension away.

At Isaiah's commissioning, God allowed the prophet to eavesdrop on an angelic anthem, "Holy, holy, holy is the Lord Almighty" (6:3). The song fired Isaiah's courageous commitment, "Here am I. Send me!" (v. 8). That music sung by the heavenly choir so profoundly impacted Isaiah that he could never be the same again, nor did he want to be. And in every new generation the song keeps affecting everyone who reads Isaiah's prophecies.

A choir from another world changed the course of human events when it interrupted the routine of a small band of unsophisticated Bethlehem sheepherders. The shepherds were terrified at first by the singing birth announcement, but as they listened more intently, they rejoiced in the life-changing message: "I bring you good news of great joy that will be for all the people. Today in the town of David a Savior has been born to you; he is Christ the Lord" (Luke 2:10-11). Then the heavenly choir added a magnificent finale, "Glory to God in the highest, and on earth peace to men on whom his favor rests" (v. 14).

That cradle song for the infant Christ so affected those first-century ranchers that they deserted their flocks, hurried to the manger, worshiped the Child, and went out to tell about their discoveries. From firsthand experience they learned it is utterly impossible to be the same after hearing angelic hymns about Jesus. On that first Christmas, the Baby set the world singing, and the music has never stopped.

Years later, Jesus hosted the Twelve at an evening meal in a borrowed upstairs dining room. There Christ washed feet, broke bread, predicted His betrayal, and led them in singing a closing hymn. Before they finished eating, Jesus sadly announced, "One of you will betray me." With bewildering confusion each one inquired, "Surely not I?" Then the Master explained, "It is one of the Twelve, one who dips bread into the bowl with me" (Mark 14:18-20). Because all had eaten with Him, the idea suddenly dawned that betrayal stands near the door of every heart. At the end of that evening, a hymn riveted the event in their minds forever.

The Passover hymn text, unknown to us, produced a profound influence on the disciples. Though they were confused in the Upper Room with closeness and separation, hope and pessimism, clarity and uncertainty, they could never get away from the impact of the song. On the night of astounding perplexity the closing hymn in the Upper Room prepared them for Gethsemane, Golgotha, the empty grave, the Emmaus walk, and Pentecost. They replayed that hymn in their hearts for the rest of their days.

Clearly, inspiring midnight songs alter the effect tragedies have on us. At Philippi, Paul and Silas were unjustly imprisoned because God answered their prayers for the healing of a demon-possessed slave girl. Her owners, having lost their profits from the girl's magic, falsely accused Paul and Silas of advocating unlawful customs. Then the preachers, after being beaten, were jailed without a legal hearing. Complaints might have been justified because they were abused and chained in stocks. The Bible, however, records a surprisingly different outcome; they sang songs that transformed their dark dungeon into a place of unforgettable victory. Instead of pianos or guitars, God accompanied their singing with an earthquake. The results amaze us even now; this heaven-inspired duet freed those unsettling street preachers from jail and saved the Roman jailer from suicide.

Well before the next sunrise, the people of God had

been given an all-time pattern for singing courage into their souls in the middle of threatening difficulties. And since then, following the inspiring example of Paul and Silas, each new generation of pilgrims in the middle of tough circumstances has sung its way to stronger faith. Spurgeon reminds us: "The Lord is the giver of our songs; He breathes the music into the hearts of His people."[3] Faith songs drive stress out of the singer's inner world.

Throughout the Bible, God uses music to celebrate His mighty works: a song welcomed creation (Job 38:7); an angel choir celebrated Christ's birth (Luke 2:14); and a jubilant hymn, "Hallelujah! For our Lord God Almighty reigns" (Rev. 19:6), is planned for the end of the world.

Dazzled by wonder and amazed by grace, the Early Church taught us by their singing how much fun it is to strike up a tune in Jesus' name in both troubling and friendly circumstances. Because Christ inspired hymn writers, poets, musicians, singers, and publishers with majestic music, neither dungeon enslavements nor Calvary's garbage heap can silence the Lord's songs for long. Singing cures stress because it reminds us that God has us completely surrounded by His care.

Hymns Teach Spirituality

Someone observed that the hymns are the poor people's poetry and the commoner's theology. Perhaps that is the reason why many churchgoers are able to quote more stanzas from the hymns than verses from the Bible. Hymns, as it has been from the earliest days of Christianity, enable disciples to understand their faith and apply it to life. That same use of gospel songs and hymns continues to make faith relevant to us in this generation.

The old hymns help us recall lessons of faith learned in our yesterdays. To sing "Jesus Loves Me" transports us back to a Sunday School class where a loving teacher taught faith lessons to a small child. To hum "Yield Not to

Temptation" renews campfire memories where teenagers were challenged to live the Christ-centered way. When memories and melodies team up, they help make doctrine applicable to life. Well beyond our awareness, an individual's beliefs are subtly but indelibly shaped by the hymns he hears and sings.

A significant fact should be added: Bible doctrine never becomes a holy energy for effective living until it becomes more than mere mental assent. Music helps make that happen. As a folk singer recently explained, an individual learns a lot about life in a short time from a song. This idea is doubly true for the music of spiritual development because hymns tie tender feelings of devotion to concepts of faith. The power of a hymn or gospel song unites faith, facts, and feelings to teach us about God.

Once touched by a hymn, one may live under its spell forever.

Spiritual Songs Take God into Ordinary Events

Hymns make it possible for spiritual pilgrims to meet God in unexpected places. A commuting executive turns his car into a sanctuary by singing, "My Jesus, I love Thee; I know Thou art mine." A jogger transforms a running track into an outdoor cathedral by playing hymns on a portable cassette player. A child's bedroom becomes a Christian learning center when a family sings Sunday School songs at bedtime. Coal miners meet God in Appalachian mines as they hum hymns. Cowboys experience divine nearness as they whistle gospel songs on their way to roundup. And a hymn sometimes transforms a hospital room into a miraculous healing place.

Who can measure what a boisterous shower solo does to the singer? A stalwart churchman's widow told me she could predict the demands on her husband's day by his morning shower songs. At the beginning of a pressing workday, he sang,

> *Stand up, stand up for Jesus . . .*
> *"Ye that are men now serve Him,"*
> *Against unnumbered foes;*
> *Let courage rise with danger,*
> *And strength to strength oppose.*
> —GEORGE DUFFIELD, JR.

He might sing on calmer days,

> *Peace, peace, wonderful peace!*
> —HALDOR LILLENAS

On a morning when he anticipated that ethical compromises needed to be faced down, he sang,

> *Consecrate me now to Thy service, Lord,*
> *By the pow'r of grace divine;*
> *Let my soul look up with a steadfast hope,*
> *And my will be lost in Thine.*
> —FANNY J. CROSBY

And at the start of a day when he expected secularism to press him, he might sing,

> *All for Jesus, all for Jesus!*
> *All my being's ransomed powers:*
> *All my thoughts and words and doings,*
> *All my days and all my hours.*
> —MARY D. JAMES

An assuring faith song transforms even a terrifying day into a victorious conquest.

Singing integrates work with worship. Dorothy Simms' broom marks rhythm for her singing in the late afternoon at San Francisco's Candlestick Park. As a member of the cleanup crew, she rakes peanut shells, Pepsi cups, and hot dog wrappers toward the aisles after athletic events. But she sings gospel songs a cappella as she sweeps empty bleachers. Though her singing is usually heard by only a few people, the wind off San Francisco Bay occasionally carries her musical message across the stadium to the press box or into the heart of a fellow worker. The size of her audience makes no difference because she is really singing love songs to God.

While singing songs of hope and affirmation in any setting, the importance of what the song can do to the singer is brought into clear focus by Thomas Merton's insight: "The hymns themselves become the Tabernacle of God in which we are protected forever from the rage of the city of business, from the racket of human opinions, from the wild carnival we carry in our hearts which the ancients called Babylon."[4] Spiritual songs protect sojourners from secularism's slavery.

Consequently, one's perspective comes into clearer focus as stress is sung away; it can happen anywhere at any time. I played a hymn in my mind before a recent trip as I waited in a busy airport ticket line amid the usual Monday morning travel confusion. To replace frustration caused by slow service and long lines, I replayed a solo I heard in church the previous day:

> *My faith has found a resting-place,*
>   *Not in device nor creed;*
> *I trust the Ever-living One,*
>   *His wounds for me shall plead.*
> *I need no other argument,*
>   *I need no other plea;*
> *It is enough that Jesus died,*
>   *And that He died for me.*
>   —LIDIE H. EDMUNDS

Later, as the jet climbed to 35,000 feet on an incredibly beautiful flying day, the clouds, mountains, and plains inspired me to sing:

> *This is my Father's world:*
>   *I rest me in the thought*
> *Of rocks and trees, of skies and seas—*
>   *His hand the wonders wrought.*
>   —MALTBIE D. BABCOCK

Then, while other passengers seemed nervous as we circled in a holding pattern over Chicago's O'Hare Airport, I recalled another song:

> *Frail children of dust, and feeble as frail,*
> *In Thee do we trust, nor find Thee to fail.*
> *Thy mercies how tender! how firm to the end!*
> *Our Maker, Defender, Redeemer, and Friend!*
> —ROBERT GRANT

The songs of faith nourished me that day as they transformed a routine flight to the Windy City into a vibrant encounter with God. These hymns sent me into my day with joy.

Carried in the heart, hymns, like prayers, make possible instant communication with God. Cruise ships, well-known for pleasure and gambling, are not usually considered to be an effective setting for worship. But once, a little after midnight, a song led me to an inexpressible meeting with God on the deck of a cruise ship. The full harvest moon, the gentle breezes, and the balmy temperature provided a reassuring testimony of the Creator's astounding extravagance. The wind, moon, and stars seemed to join me in singing,

> *To God be the glory—great things He hath done!*
> *So loved He the world that He gave us His Son.*
> —FANNY J. CROSBY

That night I understood what Augustine meant when he said a singing person prays twice: once with words and again with music.[5]

With memories to recall the texts and stereo systems to play the tunes, we find profound satisfaction in living out G. B. Stevens' translation of Eph. 5:19, "Edify one another with devout songs of praise to Christ, accompanied by the melody of the heart."[6]

Making music in the heart bonds serious pilgrims to God.

Spiritual Songs Invigorate Passages

In recent years, psychologists have discovered that adults, like children, pass through predictable human development stages. These adult transitions, to borrow Charles M. Sell's explanation, feel like leaving solid ground to travel from one island to another, so life is "described by prepositions rather than by nouns. Life is en route; to, from, into, out of, through. Fixed points are few, transitions many."[7] Though confusion is common in each new passage, songs of faith can develop assurance and affirm abiding convictions about God at each stage.

For a new young adult, leaving home—a promising though painful step—intertwines uncertainties about friendship, intimacy, vocation, and faith. For the first time, young adults experience the dread of loneliness, fear of failure, or work-related stress. What a wonderful time to sing "Oh, How He Loves You and Me" or "God Will Take Care of You." Significant possibilities become much clearer when we sing,

> *The closer I walk, the sweeter He seems.*
> *Much fairer is He than all of my dreams.*
> *His love lights my way when pathways are dim,*
> *The closer I walk to Him.**
> —HALDOR LILLENAS

Marriage, the healthy kind, fulfills a long list of identity and intimacy needs. This mysterious adventure of building a satisfying relationship with a mate is richly resourced when we sing, "O give us homes built firm upon the Savior, / Where Christ is Head and Counselor and Guide" (Barbara B. Hart). Songs like that help grow good marriages.

A pregnancy, a significant change point, adds difficult or delightful dimensions to a marriage. The developing

---

*Copyright 1931. Renewed 1959 by Lillenas Publishing Co.

new life forces a couple to repeat the human drama that has been previously experienced by millions. As the prospective father speeds through traffic to take his wife to the hospital, he keeps thinking, I'm not ready to be a parent, while the expectant mother grapples with conflicts of fear and joy. Then, at a time when stability is needed more than ever before, is a good time to sing:

> *Happy the home where Jesus' name*
> *Is sweet to ev'ry ear;*
> *Where children early lisp His fame,*
> *And parents hold Him dear.*
> —HENRY WARE, JR.

While awaiting the birth of one of our sons, my wife and I endured six months of panic-producing medical reports. Doctors frightened us with test results that said the baby would be retarded if he survived. In the midst of this cruelly unrelenting stress, strength to go on came from a minister's solo at a clergy conference:

> *Sweet is the promise—"I will not forget thee."*
> *Nothing can molest or turn my soul away;*
> *E'en though the night be dark within the valley,*
> *Just beyond is shining one eternal day.*
> *Trusting the promise, "I will not forget thee,*
> *Onward will I go with songs of joy and love.*
> —CHARLES H. GABRIEL

Soon the stress ended when a healthy son arrived. But today after more than 30 years, the song's promise is as real as this morning's sunrise.

Another difficult transition appears when a couple faces the simultaneous demands of career ascendancy and raising school-age children. Life is made chaotic by Little League, homework, car pools, school demands, and the parents' vocational responsibilities. A song for such a busy period draws us close to the Savior:

> *In the calm of the noontide, in sorrow's lone hour,*
> *In times when temptation casts o'er me its power;*
> *In the tempest of life, on its wide, heaving sea,*
> *Thou blest "Rock of Ages," I'm hiding in Thee.*
> —WILLIAM O. CUSHING

In the middle years, marked by empty nests, declining energies, and evidences of aging, some lose their way when unrealized dreams stalk their trail. Like repeating adolescence, individuals in this period sometimes second-guess issues that should have been settled forever. This passage point, when morality, meaning, and money collide, affords a good time to sing:

> *Search me, O God, and know my heart today;*
> *Try me, O Savior, know my thoughts, I pray.*
> *See if there be some wicked way in me;*
> *Cleanse me from every sin, and set me free.*
> —J. EDWIN ORR

Green winter, the aging period, demands adaptive grit. An elderly, well-adjusted friend told me he believes it is the most difficult period of all—a time when one misses being needed and friends are gone. Another senior described this stage as a time when a person starts acting more and more like himself. Loneliness, infirmities, and the funerals of friends are frightening components of these harvest years. What better time to sing hymns of hope and trust.

With uncanny realism, W. D. McGraw, my friend and father-in-law, planned his own funeral. Because he knew it was his last changing of the seasons and because the Christian faith was his lodestar, he recorded a hymn solo to be played at his funeral. On the cassette recording he invited his family and friends to join him in singing our inheritance:

> *When peace like a river attendeth my way,*
> *When sorrows like sea-billows roll;*
> *Whatever my lot, Thou hast taught me to say,*
> *"It is well, it is well with my soul."*
> —Horatio G. Spafford

Getting ready for an exam, especially the last one, is serious business. My special friend, Bob Benson, changed worlds in his middle 50s after an extraordinary ministry hounded by poor health. As he came down the homestretch, he was ushered into heaven by a friend singing at his bedside:

> *Blessed assurance, Jesus is mine!*
> *Oh what a foretaste of glory divine! . . .*
> *Perfect submission, perfect delight!*
> *Visions of rapture now burst on my sight;*
> *Angels descending bring from above*
> *Echoes of mercy, whispers of love.*
> —Fanny J. Crosby

What an affirming send-off! And what a welcome he must have enjoyed at the Father's house.

Hymns and spiritual songs help us triumphantly face each adult passage. Could it be that the hymns are really adult lullabies given by God to inspire us to live out our faith in every situation?

How to Sing Stress Away

When we begin singing, stress evaporates as the hymns and gospel songs rejuvenate us. A few uncomplicated techniques will help us sing faith into the details of our lives. Here are several starting steps.

1. Personalize the Hymn Texts. In every hymn or gospel song you hear, search for personal teaching and applications. Be ready for God to speak through the music. Ask yourself during congregational singing or choral renditions how this song speaks to your situation. Jealously guard against singing ideas that you do not mean, such as "I'll go where You want me to go, dear Lord," or "A tent or a cottage, why should I care?"

As you open your mind to these personal messages, so attractively wrapped in musical packages, you will be amazed how many songs speak to your situation. As an example, few people can remain unmoved when they apply Charles Wesley's assurance hymn to life:

> *Thou, O Christ, art all I want;*
>   *More than all in Thee I find;*
> *Raise the fallen, cheer the faint,*
>   *Heal the sick, and lead the blind.*
> *Just and holy is Thy name,*
>   *I am all unrighteousness;*
> *False and full of sin I am,*
>   *Thou art full of truth and grace.*

2. Play Hymns in Your Mind During Difficult Times. Hum hymns of affirmation in periods of suffering or loss. Whistle tunes to strengthen courage in times of fearful ambiguity. Allow memory, even in the midst of frustrating circumstances, to take you to a moment when a hymn affirmed your confidence in God or moved you to worthy action. Then when overwhelming stress comes, sing lyrics in your inner world like

> *Jesus never fails. . . .*
> *Heaven and earth may pass away,*
> *But Jesus never fails.**
>   —ARTHUR A. LUTHER

He never has and He never will.

3. Sing Aloud with Gusto. Singing aloud is a surprisingly effective way to imprint a song's message on your heart. There is nothing that focuses a day on God any bet-

---

*Copyright 1927. Renewal 1955 by A. A. Luther. Assigned to Singspiration, Inc. All rights reserved. Used by permission of Benson Music Group, Inc.

ter than singing a boisterous hymn in the shower. Regardless of musical ability, you can sing while driving alone in the car. Or you can sing a tune to banish blues as you walk in the rain. Think of yourself as mingling your singing with the composer of your favorite hymn. Sing your affirmations to lower stress.

4. Sing Prayers. Try singing your prayers. The hymnal, like the Bible, is filled with prayers of petition, confession, and praise. As a meaty devotional practice, try praying hymn prayers. A brief review of the hymnal's index will introduce you to many.possibilities. Begin with

> *O Thou in whose presence my soul takes delight,*
> *On whom in affliction I call,*
> *My Comfort by day and my Song in the night,*
> *My Hope, my Salvation, my All!*
> —JOSEPH SWAIN

5. Sing as You Exercise. The current exercise craze allows time for meditative singing, and a song helps dispel boredom during a workout activity. Play a hymn in your mind as you run. Whistle while you walk, or hum a hymn as you ride your bike. Housewives and househusbands can sing spiritual strength into their soul as they scrub, vacuum, or dust.

6. Ask Fellow Pilgrims to Share Their Favorite Hymns. An individual's faith journey can be traced around a few special songs that significantly affected him at unique moments in his journey. You likely have your list of favorites. Or you might ask a fellow struggler to tell you when he first became acquainted with a particular hymn such as "How Great Thou Art" or "Joyful, Joyful, We Adore Thee." Useful encouragement flows to your own inner life as you discover how a song impacted a friend's journey of faith.

7. Trace a Song's Influence in Your Life. When did you first hear "What a Friend We Have in Jesus"? Its influence started for some in childhood, but it took on special meaning for others during a time of great difficulty. Still others heard it for the first time during a worship experience or perhaps while growing up in a Christian family. It was a fortress of strength for me during teen years while I was trying to figure out who I was. During college, while visiting a rest home, I saw it transport patients across years to earlier experiences of faith. On an overseas mission visit, where I could not understand the language, I was reminded of the universal magnetism of Jesus as I recognized the melody. We even sang it at an open grave to celebrate a friend's home-going.

Nearly everyone has a favorite song of spirituality that takes him to the roots of his faith and turns him away from adult toys and secularity. Onetime editor of *Variety* Abel Green correctly observed, "To remember what each song did to you is like running through the chapters of your own autobiography."[8]

8. Use the Hymnal's Index as a Spiritual Development Resource. In the hymnbook you find hymns organized around spiritual development concepts like assurance, consolation, grace, and peace. As a resource for faith development, trace these noble thoughts and words in the hymns, study their use in the song texts, and check their definition in a Bible dictionary. This exercise will encourage you to sing profoundly important insights into the hidden corners of your soul.

9. Sing Dark Moods Away. During the black night of the soul, a flicker of the dawn's early light often comes while singing,

> *Before the hills in order stood,*
> *Or earth received her frame,*
> *From everlasting Thou art God,*
> *To endless years the same.*
> —Isaac Watts

It is almost impossible to fret or worry while singing,

> *No matter what may be the test,*
> *God will take care of you.*
> *Lean, weary one, upon His breast;*
> *God will take care of you.*
> —Civilla D. Martin

The pioneer psychologist in religion, William James, once observed, "We do not sing because we are happy; we are happy because we sing." Clearly the Psalmist knew this reality when he sang, "You will protect me from trouble and surround me with songs of deliverance" (32:7). Make it work for you—sing your stress away.

10. Listen for a Hymn's Meaning. The slogan of an Atlanta FM station—"seek the poetry and inner meaning of the music"—is an important suggestion for spiritual development. Often an unexpected moment of meaningful significance or a flash of inspiration comes as you listen intensely to a song of faith. When you discover a hymn's inner meaning, hold the inspiration in your heart to allow the beauty, goodness, and adventure to heal your stress. The Psalmist calls us to "rejoice in the Lord and be glad, you righteous; sing, all you who are upright in heart!" (32:11). God provides liberation through music even when stress has us pinned to the mat.

> "It is difficult to live in this present, ridiculous to live in the future, and impossible to live in the past. Nothing is as far away as one minute ago."
>
> —Jim Bishop

7

MAKE TIME YOUR FRIEND

Clocks, schedules, and calendars scramble our thinking about the good life, so we work to get more done in less and less time. Time tricks us as it races on some days like a marathon runner but loiters like a lazy bum on other days. Overcrowded schedules make us feel like Jeffy in the Family Circus cartoon, "Whenever I can't wait until tomorrow, it is yesterday." These love/hate frustrated feelings were captured by a hick radio announcer when he opened the country radio station one morning with the unnerving remark, "If you are lucky, you get a little older every day." All these topsy-turvy misgivings make us anxious about the past and afraid of the future. Many think of time as an uncontrollable monster, while others believe they benefit from fast-passing time because it forces them to weed out trivia.

This predicament, life running too slow or too fast, confuses all of us. It makes a night pass at a snail's pace for an insomniac, yet next Christmas seems like 100 years away for the little girl next door. That explains why 5 years in the future seem like tomorrow to a busy executive. That is why high school graduation sounds like light-years away for a kindergartner, while those 12 years will pass like an eye blink for the child's grandmother. These riddles underscore how an hour crawls dreadfully slow in the dentist's chair but flies incredibly fast under a romantic moon. For most of us, time problems get serious at some mysterious moment near the end of childhood when life shifts into high gear.

These frightening time puzzles are reflected in Michael Quoist's prayer, "Lord, you must have made some error in your calculation. There is a big mistake somewhere. The hours are too short, the days are too short, our lives are too short."[1] Apparently many think life would be considerably less complicated if they had more time because they feel as if they are falling behind as they strive to get ahead. As we meet ourselves coming and going, time must be seen as an ally to cultivate rather than an adversary to fight.

Time's Baffling Quirks

Time, the raw material of everything, has many fascinating quirks. Time heals wounds, equalizes many things, and is always in short supply. Trying to make sense of these beguiling distortions, Frederick Buechner remarked, "So often for many of us—all of us, really—life floats in one eye and out the other. If you asked me what I did yesterday, I'd find it hard to tell you."[2] Like a frantic seamstress, time specializes in alterations.

Though everyone knows time is the basic stuff for building a satisfying life, long years do not guarantee a meaningful existence, and fast-lane living gets us to the end too soon.

All these eccentricities keep us guessing. Every minute has 60 seconds, every day has 24 hours, and every year has 365 days—it is supposed to be the same for everyone. But time allocations are grossly unfair to those who die at 20 compared with those who live past 80.

On the opposite end of the spectrum, a recent scientific survey of 5,000 adults shows Americans have more free time than ever. A contradictory survey shows that leisure time has shrunk by 37 percent since 1973 and that the average workweek has jumped to 47 hours.

The confusion deepens more when we consider how a person squanders minutes and days but cannot hoard, earn, or borrow an hour. Time can be spent but not bought, saved but not stockpiled, given but never loaned. Time can be remembered but not reversed. You can waste a lifetime but not create a minute.

This freakish irony intensifies: Time waits for no one, but nobody knows where it goes. We stew over questions about time, like, Why do we work so hard? Why are we out of breath when we have dryers for our clothes, cars for our travel, and computers to streamline our businesses? What happened to the timesaving promises of fax machines, robotics, and other wizardries? What causes this time famine?

Our bafflement shows in the amazing custom of presenting gold watches to retirees who no longer need to keep track of time. Though it takes only a short time to live a lifetime, the average person wastes enough hours in a decade to earn a college degree.

Acceleration, among the most compelling stress-producing issues in contemporary society, means moderns sprint for planes, push ahead in supermarket lines, and fume in rush hour traffic. Our timesaving gadgets fast-forward, dub, split-screen, and record—things we never even imagined 20 years ago. In this dizzying state of affairs, the marketplace is cluttered with time management gimmicks like trendy datebooks, beguiling organizational calendars, expensive high-tech watches, confusing minicomputers, and intensive time management seminars. Yet in spite of all this bustle, time eludes us; so we are forced to agree with an unknown writer's conclusion, "Time is like a circus; always packing up and moving away."

Delusions and false assumptions fog the facts about time while our so-called shortcut schedules fill every minute to the brim. We are captives to our cellular phones, answering machines, and personal computers plus the time requirements of our greed to earn more money to buy things we do not need. All this makes us chuckle when we read the hotel elevator sign, "This is the tomorrow you worried about yesterday." As we consider the issue, our own rat race makes us nod in agreement with the anonymous pessimist who penciled at the bottom of the sign, "Now we know why."

Convincing indicators can be seen everywhere that real satisfaction depends on whether we choose to make time our adversary or friend.

What Is Time For?

Time, the landscape of experience,[3] according to Francis Bacon, might be considered to be the bricks and lumber for building a life of satisfying achievements and fulfilling relationships. That means stress-causing irritations are constantly felt by those who think they have too much or too little time—which includes nearly everybody.

Surprisingly, the determining cause of this stress appears to be inside an individual; two people have similar jobs, but one is relaxed with enough time for work and play while the other is breathlessly busy. Though nearly everyone knows, what we do with time is more important than its duration; family time, mealtime, sick time, and marriage time are out of control for many people. Consequently, the desired finished product—a satisfying life—gets squeezed to the ragged edges because adequate time is seldom allocated for reflection, creativity, or God.

If all of this is accurate, the complications of our busyness can be lessened when we cultivate time as a cherished friend rather than fearing it as a threatening taskmaster. Though such a decision appears to be easy to make, it is actually revolutionary because it is the first step toward viewing time as a gem to treasure, a joy to give, or even a luxury to squander. However, no combination of gadgets, innovations, or helpful insights will automatically nurture a friendship with time.

Perhaps it is time to wake up to what our compulsions about schedules and calendars are doing to us. At some point an individual must consider the toll busyness takes on his emotions and spirit. It is amazing, but true, that the spiritual development side of living must become a genuine priority before we can accurately decide what else is important to us.

As those alternatives are considered, we are likely to be attracted to the Jesus way, which Pastor Milo Arnold explains in this two-sentence insight: "Jesus didn't need longer days nor extended years. He just took the time He had and fitted life into it so well that His work was done when His time was gone."[4] Clearly, our Lord never postponed a task because of lack of time, but what a satisfying life He lived. Jesus stands as a worthy model for effective use of time.

Quality time is the price one pays for meaning. To begin developing a friendship with time, one starts by sorting out the difference between hurry and satisfaction. The two may be miles apart. Gandhi, the Hindu statesman, understood this point: "There is more to life than increasing its speed."[5] Our task, therefore, is to find ways to live better rather than packing more activities into our overstuffed calendars.

Perhaps the most basic ingredient for building a quality life is to recognize that each time segment has incredible potential for fulfillment, and schedules cannot control us without our consent. Thus weary, overstressed people must reverse their ideas about being prisoners of time. Time does not chase us with a dagger, nor does it hold us as captive slaves.

Strange as it seems, the whole world can get along without us for five minutes or longer; it did before our birth, and it will probably survive after we are gone.

To begin thinking in new ways, why not consider time to be a basket filled with fulfillment possibilities and renewal power? Commit to the liberating notion that going back will never take us forward. Plainly, then, new days, new weeks, and new seasons will remind us that we live surrounded by fresh beginnings that contain potential to lower stress and help us get better acquainted with God. This is the precise reason why it is important to occasionally step off the whirling treadmill to catch our breath, to nurture our soul, and to put our ear close to life so that we can hear what God says about our use of time through a thousand different voices.

Time Enough for What Really Matters

Squandered minutes waste life. Carl Sandburg, the two-time Pulitzer prize poet, points out an uncomfortable thought about our mind-numbing schedules: "Time is the coin of your life. It is the only coin you have and only you can determine how it will be spent. Be careful lest you let others spend it for you."[6] Though life without intentional control evaporates like water on desert sand, few people seem able to do much about it.

Thoughtful decisions must be made about one's use of time for two reasons: (1) it is your personal possession—it belongs only to you, and (2) it is limited—no one can get more time.

Consequently, the way one prioritizes time guarantees there will be few dull moments for those who use it well. A quality life takes time; a satisfying life takes more time; and a great life takes even more time. That is why the Old Testament writer of Ecclesiastes believed everything has an ideal time, and the accuracy of his insight eventually dawns on every serious seeker after God. The idea is amplified in poetic language by dramatist Edmund Rostrand: "There is a time when beauty stands staring into the soul with sad, sweet eyes that sicken at the sounds of words. And God help those who pass that moment by."[7]

Building a happy relationship with time determines whether we stagger through life or journey with a satisfying purpose toward meaning. Indeed, every time segment, however short or long, possesses marvelous possibilities for living fully and hopefully. Time is yours; only truly significant issues are worth large investments of your time.

Models for Making Friends with Time

Let me introduce several common though extraordinary people who cultivated a happy friendship with time by refusing to squander the bits and pieces of their lives. Though they probably never read George Bernard Shaw's writings, they embraced his idea that the greatest joy is to be used up by a purpose you recognize as a mighty one.[8]

Martin Paulson chose in retirement years to be a substitute grandfather to my preschool sons, who lived hundreds of miles from natural grandparents. These boys, now grown men, learned how to saw and hammer from Grandfather Paulson. Beyond that they experienced the delightful fringe benefit of a spellbinding relationship with an adult friend. Martin intuitively followed Paul's advice, "Let love guide your life" (Col. 3:14, TLB). Who can calculate his impact on the children or measure his fulfillment in giving them the gift of himself?

In their late 20s, Margie and Paul Kemp moved into cramped University of Michigan campus housing with three grade-school-age sons to pursue education degrees that earlier seemed unimportant. Later, after years of classroom teaching and earning advanced degrees, Paul was promoted to a high-level educational post where he continues as an influential key player in formulating public school policy affecting thousands of children. Margie, in her too-short lifetime, worked miracles with speech-handicapped preschool children, so that some of her so-called learning disabled kids have since graduated with honors from college. By investing in children, Margie and Paul learned that immense satisfaction is a spin-off of giving time away. In the process they made the world better.

Madge Watson, after a long career as an administrative assistant to a Holly Sugar Corporation executive, thought retirement wasted her time. Well beyond 65, she became a girl Friday for a small church, where she operated a temperamental copy machine, answered phone calls, and replied to hundreds of questions about the church-operated preschool. On purpose, Madge used her senior years to discover a gratifying life unknown to many people.

Following the leukemia death of his 20-year-old daughter, Wayne Sparling, master metal craftsman, took massive chunks of time from his thriving business to design, build, and install a steeple for his church as productive grief work. His time gift became a fitting tribute to Nancy's life because his work of art will draw the community and church closer to God for years into the future. Who can compute the impact of his time gift?

Like Martha of the Bible, Clara Underwood served the senior adults of her church and gave special attention to Elizabeth Cullin during her long, losing battle with cancer. Clara, equally at home in her garden or a sickroom, took a homegrown rose to Mrs. Cullin every day and practiced her conviction that time is a strength to be given to those who need it most.

Mary Quackenbush refused to allow advancing years to slow her down to a life of respectable ease. After renewing her faith commitment at 75, she started out on a 12-year period of effort for Christ where she became a well-loved spiritual mother to an entire congregation. She packed each week full of blissful service by counting the church offerings on Monday, sponsoring a Bible study for mature women in her home on Tuesday, calling on lonely hospitalized people all day Wednesday, leading a visitation team on Thursday evenings, and teaching a Bible class for preteen girls on Sunday mornings. She added vigor to her years by serving others.

From firsthand experience, these people found Jesus'

teaching to be time-consuming but satisfying: "Whoever wants to become great among you must be your servant" (Mark 10:43). They deepened friendships with time by giving it away. Equally significant, they invested large time blocks in the servanthood ideal of Jesus as a satisfying way to develop a happy relationship with time.

A Good Life or a Crowded Datebook

The famous family matriarch Rose Kennedy once observed, "Crowding a life does not always enrich it."[9] She is right. Unnerving as it seems, an unexamined, frantic life-style feeds on itself to create a series of self-sustained frustrations.

Often we fool ourselves into believing that outside forces are responsible for our overfull lives. For some strange reason, being able to blame someone or something seems to end the discussion and frees us from making necessary adjustments. After all, this line of reasoning says, it is difficult to face the issue that no outward force ultimately determines how we spend our time. The argument continues, how could we be responsible when we are victimized by the expectations of others and helplessly out of breath? But we are.

To get life on track, start with a straightforward admission that clocks and calendars are helpful servants but never uncontrollable slave drivers. To deal with these issues, time questions must be asked, like, How can I make my life count? What needs to be done? How can I do it? Who really needs me?

More careful attention to intensity and urgency furnishes bold initiatives for cultivating this desired friendship. Robert S. Eliot's compelling questions help clarify the intensity and urgency concerns: If I knew I had only six months to live, (1) what do I have to do, (2) what do I want to do, and (3) what are the things I neither have to do nor want to do?[10] Another approach is to evaluate each time demand by assigning it one of three categories: trivial, important, or essential. Using either technique automatically forces introspection, which helps us choose what we really want to do with this priceless commodity called time. Remember, nothing is as momentous as it appears at first.

Like nourishing any relationship, this budding companionship requires reassignments of seconds, minutes, and days. Some time management authorities believe this is difficult to achieve simply because only about 5 percent of our time is uncommitted. Therefore, before any new commitments are made, ask yourself what adjustments you are willing to make and what adjustments can you make? A half-hour investment in Bible reading requires another interest must release 30 minutes. An evening at home requires another commitment for the same night be given up. Likewise, a two-day prayer retreat means 48 hours must be taken from something else. Bob Benson offers insightful direction for these realignments: "If you will ask God what He would do if it were His life, He would gladly tell you."[11]

Thus, constant monitoring is needed to work toward a balanced life even when priorities become temporarily blurred, as they will. Robert Wood's prayer sharpens the distinctions between a crowded schedule and a fulfilled life:

Almighty God, teach me timing . . .
There are times in my life to plant
 an idea in the mind of an inquisitive child,
 a seed of hope for someone in need,
 the gift of trust in one birthing faith.
There are times in our lives
 to scatter stones that build walls,
 to gather stones that build bridges between individuals.
Teach us the times to seek
 out the fellowship of the body of Christ,
 the solitude of meditation,
 to serve others with humility and love . . .[12]

Cloisters and Saints on the Run

Christian history records unnumbered pilgrims who withdrew to cloisters to cultivate pious lives and gain control over the details of life. At the quiet place, they discovered spiritual energy, which enabled them to produce the literature of the inner life and recuperate from stress. True to these satisfying discoveries, they recommend lengthy withdrawal from anything or anyone that drains us of spiritual vitality. Their advice feels good to us because all sojourners occasionally hunger for some facet of the cloistered life to slow their feverish pace and to fill their inner emptiness.

As radio commentator Paul Harvey would say, "Now for the rest of the story." What about activists so involved in serving others that they never took time to write their findings? One spiritual formation writer correctly observed: "Jesus was a holy man . . . There were times He had to be alone with the Father. But I am beginning to believe that His holiness did not come because He withdrew from life; He was holy because He entered into life at every level."[13] Could the reason we know so little about spiritual activists be that they never found enough time to record their insights and experiences?

Before activists are dismissed as unimportant, we must consider how impoverished the world would be without superactive saints who dash through life with a prayer on their lips and a Bible in their hands. Examples are around us everywhere—some obvious but others almost unnoticed. Patience Hole, lady pastor of the housechurch of my childhood in Detroit, was a busy mother in Christ to her little flock—loving, caring for, and affirming us. Charles Hoos, while living in a hectic world like ours, functioned as a father and mother to his children, remodeled the church with his own hammer, baked birthday cakes, washed clothes, visited hospitals, demonstrated Christian compassion to the needy, and preached powerfully to human needs. Archie Woodward, evangelist and longtime family friend, kept a schedule that put him in such close touch with people that he was ready on a moment's notice to sing, pray, preach, play softball, or ride a motorcycle. J. V. Morsch, our pastor and friend during our family's first immediate encounter with death, was and is a whirlwind for God. These active souls and thousands like them honed their spiritual growth on the anvil of selfless service for God and for their fellow human beings.

There can be no doubt that faith often prospers in the cloistered life, but God also travels busy roads with His activists. Maybe pioneer spiritual literature writers and more modern disciples put too much distance between action and contemplation. Maybe we do too. A fulfilled life needs both. At certain periods withdrawal may be most needed, but at other times an exhilarating commitment to action is required.

In speaking of this balance, James C. Fenhagen, the Episcopal priest and theological educator, says of the apostle Paul, "His activism was the fruit of the relationship he enjoyed with the living Christ."[14] This interplay between thought and action builds on the fact that busy Marthas and meditative Marys are both needed and cherished in Bible times and throughout the church's history. A balance like that is needed now.

Lived-out devotion is wonderfully nourished by a rhythm of solitude and service or waiting and doing. God shows himself in the crowded moments of our lives, but He appears in the quiet times too. Catherine de Hueck Doherty calls us to aspire to both: "Because you are more aware of God, because you have been called to listen in your inner silence, you can bring God to the street, the party, the meeting, in a powerful way."[15] Consequently, there is no reason for believers to choose between reflection and action; both intensify our aliveness and usefulness. Meditation and prayer are the winds of God that drive the sails of spirituality to take us out into the deep places of adventuresome service and long-term satisfaction.[16]

Making Time for Faith Formation

Our perplexities about time keep changing throughout the transitions of life. Mothers-to-be think pregnancies will never end. Young parents wonder if babies will ever grow up.

Middle-aged couples long for grown children to come home more often. Cancer victims often have trouble deciding whether time moves too fast or too slow for them. Elderly people, with time to spare, long for more visits from friends. Nearly everyone, regardless of age or vocation, wishes he could change his supply of time; most people want more time, and a few want less. Such changes are impossible.

Since this is true, the solution seems to be in making better use of the time already available to us. Think of the life-changing possibilities in a one-minute contact with God. In an "aha" sentence, Carstens and Mahedy suggest, "Many people find it surprisingly difficult to concentrate for a full minute on a single subject."[17] Amazing as it sounds, even when a month is available to consider a job change or a marriage proposal, no one spends all 43,200 minutes on that concern.

Our own experience supports this idea that even when faced with serious choices, we only think about a specific issue for a few minutes several times each day. Therefore, Carstens and Mahedy conclude correctly, "Sound decisions or solutions to problems emerge from long stretches of intermittent consideration with the active part done about one minute at a time."[18] The significance of this idea is obvious—there is more time available for decisions and faith formation than we think. The missing ingredients may be that we have not allowed choice, love for a cause, and passion for a commitment to shape our time allocations.

Everyone has more frequent short-time segments available for faith formation than he thinks. The proposal to use fleeting time periods for spiritual development is not new. Fénelon, the French spirituality pilgrim, suggested years ago: "We must often raise our heart to God. . . . All the most preoccupied moments are good times, even while eating and hearing others talk."[19] This concept shows God seekers that street corners, quiet walks, fast freeways, and even boring committee meetings offer effective time frames for encountering God. More situations can be used as productive opportunities for spiritual development than we have yet imagined.

Gear Up for Golden Moments

People easily forget routine happenings but remember epic moments forever. A contemporary author who understands life suggests, "If you throw your arms around such a moment and hug it like crazy, it may save your soul."[20] Everyone has at least one impressive tale about a golden experience he never wants to forget. But each minute must be lived to the full to keep ready for these golden moments.

No one knows why a special moment happens when it does, and few people are fully aware when they are making a memory. But time is the basic ingredient of a never-to-be-forgotten moment. For a small boy to build a Cub Scout Soap Box Derby racing car means someone must invest time to teach him to use woodworking tools. For a college student to earn academic honors means some teacher invested large time commitments in his education. For salty sea breezes to blow through a crippled senior citizen's snow-white hair means someone coordinated the time-consuming logistics to get her on the houseboat. Every unforgettable experience demands that someone make significant time commitments to a cause or a person.

The possible variety is amazing. An unforgettable experience can sneak up on a parent as he talks with a little child. A glorious moment may show up as a surprising payoff for an apparently insignificant task done at church. Sometimes, a dawn of meaning breaks in on an average day. Or it may come during a chance meeting of old friends. Tasting the passing moment fully,[21] to borrow from the French novelist Camus, may happen anytime or anywhere. Keep ready for the memory of it, and be prepared to pay for a lovely moment by enjoying it.[22]

God often sends these moments across the spiritual development bridges of worship, prayer, and service. Buechner is right: "In the final analysis, all moments are key moments, and life itself is grace."[23] Though momentous happenings cannot be orchestrated, they never take place without flexible time commitments and active curiosity.

These golden moments, however, are so delightful that no one wants to miss even one. To multiply the possibilities, famous author James A. Michener suggests, "Don't put off for tomorrow what you can do today, because if you enjoy it today you can do it again tomorrow."[24]

Robert J. Hastings tells how to keep ready for memorable moments: "Stop pacing the aisles and counting the miles. Instead, climb more mountains, eat more ice cream, go barefoot oftener, swim more rivers, watch more sunsets, laugh more, and cry less. Life must be lived as we go along."[25] The secret—savor each moment, search for its significance, and hug the memory to your heart.

This zestful openness required to relish golden moments shows in John Henry Jowett's prayer: "My Father, give me a sense of the unspeakable value of time. May I so live as to place a jewel in every moment."[26]

The Sanskrit proverb shows us how:
> Look to this day
> For yesterday is but a dream,
> And tomorrow is only a vision,
> But today, well lived,
> Makes every yesterday a dream of happiness
> And every tomorrow a vision of hope.
> Look well, therefore, to this day.[27]

Keep Committed to the Present

Though not thinking about spirituality, U.S. President Lyndon B. Johnson once observed that most people put second things first.[28] He is right; nobody knows why, we just do. This natural tendency shows in our focus on a spent past or an uncertain future; all those hankerings must be resisted and corrected. Scripture announces an important reality to aid us: "Jesus Christ," as Lord over everything including time, "is the same yesterday, today, and forever" (Heb. 13:8, TLB); and that makes the present moment special, useful, and redemptive.

Since the present makes up the "good ol' days" we will dearly treasure tomorrow, why not enjoy them now? Yesterday is behind you, the rest of your life is ahead. Therefore, we cannot allow ourselves to waste the present dimension of life, since it is the only part of time we actually have.

Yet thousands allow themselves to be trapped waiting for unclear tomorrows, and they look at life mostly through rearview mirrors. Their regrets handcuff them to the past, while their fear about the future makes them hostage to problems that may never happen. This life-squandering process squeezes all the significance out of today. Columnist Ann Landers explains the risk, "One of these days may be none of these days."[29] She has the situation sized up accurately. Without vigilance, the miracle of enjoying the present blessings never happens.

To be present in the present may take more than a rational attempt to adjust the focus away from the past or the future. One remedy is to apply the Jesuit priest Jean de Caussade's enlightening phrase "sacrament of the present"[30] to life.

De Caussade's four-word phrase encourages us to put out the welcome mat to the indescribable potential of the present. That word *sacrament* shines a clear light on making the present a good place to be and brings helpful attitudes to mind—like worshipful awe, a holy remembrance, a new start, an undeserved gift, a means of grace, or even a mystery from God. His idea pushes us to seize the present so that we can fill each moment with meaning. This sacramental notion also reminds us graphically of what we already know—God stands ready to infuse the present moment with more possibilities than we can imagine. Then life need never feel like an empty cup, a dead-end street, or a barren wilderness.

Cherishing the present moment enough to use it well adds zest to the spiritual journey. Writing in the autumn of her life, Sarah Patton-Boyle explains the rewards of a refocus on the present: "The world around me began to sparkle and shine. I perceived sunlight in a different way. Flowers, trees, clouds, the richly varied music of nature and of man rounded out and became full. In my marrow and muscle, I felt the sometimes hastening, sometimes plodding energy of all living things."[31] For our own good, we must desert our illusions about the future and refuse to allow the past to be a deadly shrine. Celebrate the present for its potential and grace; that will fill tomorrow's memories concerning today full of peace.

In small, significant ways we carry an imprint of each day on our mind and memory wherever we go and whatever we do. Though few realize it, every unlived day irrevocably impacts the future in some way, even as each kindly deed and expression of love enriches every tomorrow. Clearly, if we are to make friends with time and lower stress, Paul's teaching must be heeded in the present, "Take time and trouble to keep yourself spiritually fit" (1 Tim. 4:7, Phillips).

Guidance for present-tense living shines through this anonymous poem:

Today is ours—let's live it.
And love is strong—let's give it.
A song can help—let's sing it.
And peace is dear—let's bring it.
The past is gone—don't rue it.
Our work is here—let's do it.
The world is wrong—let's right it.
If evil comes—let's fight it.
The road is rough—let's clear it.
The future vast—don't fear it.
Is faith asleep?—let's wake it.
Today is free—let's take it.[32]

For a satisfying life, make the most of all time dimensions—past, present, future—by allowing God to inform your present from the past and to enrich today with hopes about tomorrow. A fulfilled life depends on our attitude toward time. Why not make time your best friend?

Making Time Your Friend

Hurry sickness can be healed, the chains of our frenzied deadlines broken, and a wonderful friendship with time can be built. One starts by mobilizing his own will. But how? How can we, with the same number of hours as everyone else, make our lives less hectic and more fulfilled? What constructive strategies can be used? About yourself, believe what John W. Gardner says about others, "Even in the most apathetic, the most materialistic, or even the most unimaginative member of a group there is something waiting to be awakened, wanting to be awakened."[33]

1. Let Done Be Done. Additional work on a complete project increases frustration and wastes time. Leave a finished assignment. Charlie Shedd reports a young career woman's self-discovery, "No wonder I'm worn out! I do everything I do so many times. First I worry about doing it—then when I have done it, I do it over, worrying whether I did it right." She has something important to teach us: give your best to a task and trust the results to God. Only the Father knows the long-term results of a deed, but He knows.

2. Boss Your Time. Scrutinize your schedule to see what your calendar says about your priorities and your performance. Does your datebook support your intended values? A dedicated cardiac surgeon places patient care ahead of golf. A serious law student considers preparation for her bar exam more important than shopping. A committed emergency room nurse is more eager to ease suffering than to complete insurance forms. An effective teacher prefers to sharpen a student's mind over leaving school early each afternoon. And some executives are downshifting voluntarily in corporate life to have more time for family and themselves. Try to be both efficient and effective.

Greater time control can be achieved by a more flexible approach to scheduling. One expert recommends allowing 25 percent more time for each task than you might expect to take; the cushion allows expanded time for each task or provides free time if the extra time is not needed. Another specialist suggests that no more than one-half of our time should be scheduled so that we allow for interruptions, unplanned demands, or creative thought—or all of them. Sadly, but not surprisingly, schedules often reveal something significantly different from the way their owner planned to use his life.

Critically analyze your calendar. Quiz your datebook to see if your priorities control your actions. Accept the fact that busyness can be used to keep you from finishing difficult assignments or facing hard decisions. Just as a checkbook assigns values to spending, a datebook assigns values to conduct.

Why not refocus your activities on essentials? Don't rush your life away.

3. Shun the Success Trap. The road to the top in any field could make you miserable. Success seldom satisfies for long; the thing we want the most often brings undesirable burdens. Fast-lane living often traps people in unsatisfying success and leaves little time for inner growth.

Many individuals, by the time they reach middle age, feel locked into a professional or corporate wilderness. Regrettably, the same possibility of overreaching ambitions exists for blue-collar workers and business owners. To avoid this trap, try evaluating your intentions against every unrelenting deadline, every struggle for prominence, and every desire for instant gratification.

A fulfilled life demands a balance between reflection and activity. Why not try to fire as much enthusiasm for interior development like prayer, meditation, and encounter with Scripture as you already feel for security, work, and hobbies. Then at the end of the day, quiet your body, center your mind, and talk with God. Surprisingly, the day's stress will ease as adventures in prayer, Scripture reading, and meditation increase.

4. Apply Disciplines to the Demands of Your Life. Like short sips of refreshing cool water, the spiritual disciplines can be used even when you are experiencing pressing time constraint. When necessary, Christ makes encouragement and enablement available to us in one-minute segments.

Even though the spiritual disciplines are as old as Christianity, these common practices such as fasting, sharing, prayer, and serious study of Scripture are useful ways to deal with the stressful frustrations of modern life. But if these traditional disciplines are to make a difference to the individual quester, they must be infused with meaning to avoid the cartoon character Ziggy's testimony, "Lately I've gotten into transcendental vegetation."

Ask yourself several key questions: What insights about the use of time do I receive from Scripture? What options for uncluttering life come to mind as I pray? How can intercession, service, and centering on Christ lessen my time stressors? What can I do to make tomorrow spiritually significant?

5. Develop a Time Log. A time log helps a person keep track of time and audit the results; it also helps an individual acknowledge ownership of time and helps him control its use. As an effective way to evaluate priorities, try keeping an activity log in 15-minute segments for a week or month, using only categories that make sense to you, like family, job, leisure, television viewing, devotional development, and worship.

Try holding yourself seriously accountable for what truly matters. Admit to yourself that your use of time ultimately determines the kind of life you live; schedule extended periods of time when you can withdraw for a change of activity, geography, and people.

6. Learn to Say No. Say no for the right reasons.

Sometimes it is difficult to resist accepting too many commitments because requests flatter us. But no one can do everything. There will be times, as you cultivate your inner life, when worthy tasks must wait for another day or somebody else. Sometimes saying no makes room in the schedule to prepare for future tasks.

Then, too, overcommitments often produce inferior work. Elton Trueblood is right, "Holy shoddy is still shoddy." When we overschedule ourselves, the quality of our service suffers, the Kingdom is weakened, and we no longer strive for excellence. No, rightly used, helps us pay closer attention to the meaning and quality of all our activities.

7. Drop "Too Busy" from Your Conversation. God never overloads anyone, even though others may make too many demands on us. When tempted to use that phrase, "too busy," ask yourself if God has given you too much to do or if you have less time than others. The Father's pace provides both fulfilling satisfaction and worthy accomplishments. And He is never impressed with a frenzied life-style even in His most pious children. Low motivation, overcommitment, poor organization, or inappropriate priorities may be the real culprits.

Try listening to the absurd things others say about time. Notice how some people talk about being busy but in the next sentence discuss watching long hours of television. Or, they may discuss the crushing demands of their job but brag the next moment about long coffee breaks.

Your conversation may sound just as amusing to others. Try to drop "too busy" from your vocabulary and harmonize your day and week around the way God directs you to use your time.

8. Hurry Up to Slow Down. Accelerate routine activities to accomplish necessary tasks more quickly. Iron faster so that you can read slower. Hurry grocery shopping so that you can pray at a leisurely pace. Wash your car quickly so that you can explore nature with a child. Step lively as you mow the lawn so that you have more time for Scripture. Rush newspaper reading so that you can take a drive to see a sunset.

Hurry routine responsibilities so that you can develop godliness in a more methodical manner. Pace yourself. What can be speeded up? What can be eliminated? What needs more attention? Effective spiritual growth usually requires a reappropriation of time.

9. Measure Life by Quality. Stop judging life by accumulations, like how many customers, clients, accounts, number of committees on which you serve, number of jobs you fill in the church, or how hard you work. Consider the comment attributed to Will Rogers, "It's not so much what you do each day—it is what you get done that counts." Since there is much to enjoy on occasions when you are not ruled by the clock, why not take off your watch on a weekend and allow yourself to be directed by your natural sense of timing? John Gardner suggests favored environments for quality life development, like a walk at the beach or a special fishing stream, and a nonverbal pastime such as music, gardening, sports, light reading, or work with one's hands.[34]

Begin thinking of satisfying relationships and quality achievement; then rid your schedule of the commitments that only feed your vanity. Take time to get better acquainted with your family. Set aside time to cultivate your inner world. Try something new to develop a growing edge to free you from the repetition of daily events; try a new sport, take a class, or begin a new hobby. Ask God to cure your hurry so that you can enjoy life more.

10. Use Jesus as a Model for Time Evaluation. Jesus taught that the road to spirituality is always under construction, and He provides us with a magnificent example for building a fulfilled life. Remember the renewal He received from withdrawal from His regular routines.

Compare the way you use your time with the way Jesus used His time during His earthly ministry. At the beginning of your day, ask yourself how many hours you are willing to place in His hands. Adjust your commitments to what He wants done. How does God judge the way you used yesterday? How does He evaluate your plans for tomorrow? Be as specific as possible because vagueness can be confusing and deadly.

As you consider the details of your living, use the petition Jesus prayed as your own, "Father, into your hands I commit my spirit" (Luke 23:46). Ask God to provide insight for developing friendship with time so that you may experience strength for weakness, peace for frustration, and confidence in place of tension. Flavia, the greeting card designer, says it so well: "Do something wonderful with this day—for it will never come again."

> *"One of the most wonderful gifts we receive from a soul friend is that of a new perspective. He or she is able to stir up our imagination so that we not only view the past differently, but also allow the future to be filled with new, exciting possibilities."*
>
> —Alan Jones

8

CHERISH RELATIONSHIPS

Once, my seminary friend Ford Miller served as a student minister at Asbury United Methodist Church in Prairie Village, Kans. One afternoon, a charming six-year-old girl answered his knock at the door of her home. After helping her mother welcome the pastor, the child called her friends into the house and tried this faltering introduction: "Pastor Miller, these are my friends. I use them every day."

Her social error sounds amusingly shocking at first, but in real life we all use friends every day because we need them so badly. Our actions, growing out of an unquenchable hunger for relationships, agree with a "Graffiti" cartoon, "Make good friends before you need them."[1] Friends, as much a part of the human legacy as our genetic makeup, provide a link with what really matters—an effective stress-reducing factor.

God puts friends and family into life to satisfy our inborn desire for closeness. He created this capacity in us to cherish each other, and He sometimes makes us see old friends in wonderful new ways. Virginia Coleman expressed affection for her church friends during a prayer meeting in this charming way, "I thank God for you. I never want to get you out of my heart." Even though most of us feel this way deep down, we are usually too preoccupied to give adequate attention to the reservoir of undeveloped or tarnished relationships that could easily be cultivated into gratifying friendships.

The need for friends is pressingly obvious; well-nourished relationships add to our wholeness and have a lot to do with keeping us emotionally and spiritually healthy. I found this wisdom on an unsigned craft plaque during a visit to the many gift shops where my wife takes me: "A friend is one who knows you as you are, understands where you've been, accepts what you have become, and still gently invites you to grow." Such tender ties blunt the damage tension does to us.

Though friendships come in varying levels of intensities, every relationship has potential to point us to God and lessen our stress. The incalculable benefits—all components of wholeness—include intangible payoffs like affection, trust, respect, mutual aid, understanding, devotion, acceptance, spontaneity, and self-disclosure.

A Latin poet underscores the incredible necessity of tearing down our self-constructed barriers so that others can come in:

> *I look for God*
> *and I cannot find God.*
> *I look for myself*
> *and I cannot find myself.*
> *But I find a friend;*
> *And the three of us*
> *We go on our way together.*[2]

Relationships—Remedy for Loneliness

Loneliness, a first cousin to stress, is so common in contemporary life that social science professionals estimate that 100 million Americans suffer from some degree of social isolation.[3] From experience, most people understand why a nightclub comedian generates a sad laughter when he jokes, "Remember, we are all in this alone." And in the same city, a pop singer sadly admitted in a newspaper interview, "I stand across the stage lights from hundreds of people when I perform, but after the show, I go to an empty room as a prisoner of success." To be all alone is among the worst despairs anyone ever feels.

Surprisingly, even those who spend their time in crowds live close to loneliness. Albert Schweitzer, the humanitarian missionary to Africa, once said we are all so much together, but we are all dying of loneliness. Though the concept sounds unbelievable, research supports the idea that most persons have fewer than 10 real friends throughout their lifetime; other informal surveys say it is 5 or less. Apparently, lots of people live with an unmet hunger to be close to others whose acceptance does not depend on what they do or say—a safe place where they can be themselves.

Yesterday, I met a man who appeared to have it all—high-paying job, flashy car, and an impressive address. But he has not seen his lifelong friends and extended family for five years because they are located back home, more than 2,500 miles away. This space and time distance cause him unbearable stress, which he loathes. This man, however, is not alone in his loneliness because he fits the pattern of thousands who are isolated by circumstances beyond their control. One of the most pressing dilemmas of our time is how to establish and sustain the enabling relationships everyone needs.

The fact that meaningful relationships keep slipping away complicates the loneliness problem. Death separates mates and friends. Betrayal breaks relationships. Divorce fractures families. Transitions, geography, or growing apart often create an ebb in the intensity of friendships. But Vernon Grounds underscores an important fact in his delightful discussion of human porcupines: "We were not made to live as a recluse, a hermit, or a lone wolf, but in fellowship with our neighbor. We were made to enter into a relationship of love and trust and service with other people. And unless we do this we become emotionally sick, miserable, and frustrated."[4]

Since satisfying associations require constant tending, this loneliness question forces seekers after meaning to rethink ways to nourish friendships. The Bible records the loneliness of stalwart people in many difficult situations: Daniel in the lions' den; Elijah under a juniper tree; John the Baptist in the desert; Paul in a Roman jail; and Jesus in the wilderness, in Gethsemane, and on the middle Cross. These examples make us realize that God is no stranger to our feelings of isolated detachment, and He stands ready with effective remedies to heal our separation from others.

However, just when loneliness feels like an inner holocaust, God reminds us, "This is ridiculous!" The remedy, already in our hearts, is that everyone can give friendship to another person, so both parties can be healed. Every human being was meant to love, touch, and be close to others.

Naturally, these efforts to build happy associations occasionally travel over a bumpy, two-way road. The cartoon caption is at least partially correct: "A circle of friends usually includes triangles and squares."[5] It is true, healthy relationships start with the tough task of accepting people as they are, but close friendships are worth every effort. Beginning at any moment, life can be enriched and stress lowered by making a conscious effort to treat everyone we meet as a potential friend.

Relationships—a Faith Development Laboratory

God created relationships as a testing ground to verify His teachings about family, friends, and church. Relationships, much more than a convenient way to organize society, provide a unique laboratory for developing spirituality, so that even when human linkages tax patience, they help us become authentic and build inner integrity. Consequently, every bridge-building effort to develop friendship offers unlimited possibilities to improve life with love given and received and often makes us see God better.

The Persian proverb offers interesting insights for developing relationships: "We come into the world crying while all [those] about us are smiling. May we live so that we go out of this world smiling while everybody around us is weeping."

Just as a scientific laboratory examines and proves theories, relationships help us validate ideas about spiritual development and cause us to recognize the unspeakable beauty of each person. John Mogabgab's summary proves accurate in human experience: "A friend whose parish is located in Detroit's inner city once observed that when you open your heart to God, you never know who the Lord will bring along."[6] In this faith development lab, forgiveness, for example, becomes as real as light. Love proves stronger than hate in this lab for living. At the same time, hope overpowers doubt.

Far from being a robot factory, these friendship laboratories demonstrate how difficult it can be to live in harmony with others without divine enablement. Consequently, the Father sends people as two-way channels for us to give and receive grace, mercy, and affirmation. Such testing teaches us a lot about God, ourselves, and others even as it forces us to consider the counsel of the 16th-century Carmelite reformer, John of the Cross, "God has so ordained things that we grow in faith only through the frail instrumentality of one another."[7]

The surprising mutual benefit that grows out of well-lived relationships must also be considered. Albert Schweitzer explains the astonishing benefits: "Not one of us knows what effect his life produces, and what he gives to others; that is hidden from us and must remain so, though we are often allowed to see some little fraction of it, so that we may not lose courage."[8] Life lived in meaningful association with others offers us a wellspring of satisfaction, while living in isolation makes us wither and die.

Friends, as special gifts from God, sustain us in dark hours, encourage us to cross-examine our delusions, and lend their support when we are afraid to believe in ourselves or God. Interestingly, others receive the same from us, so lavish benefits flow both ways. Fulfilling relationships provide fertile soil for growing robust faith and are a convenient way to lower our stress.

Friends—People Who Point Us to God

Devotional writers, preachers, theologians, and pastors all help us apply spiritual development basics like Scripture, prayer, obedience, loving, fasting, and giving to the details of life. Bob Benson, however, adds another viable and largely untapped source: "St. Ignatius Loyola taught his followers to seek and find God in all things. But with apology to the Saint, why not seek and find God in everyone."[9] Other people—anywhere, anytime—offer new ways of seeing God and life. Often God's voice can be clearly heard through close-by human beings who are unforgettable exhibits of love, grace, and forgiveness. Consequently, we must cherish and use the amazing fact that everyone we meet may have a potentially fresh insight from the Father for us.

Friends nourish faith. The endless possibilities can come from unexpected sources. Noble deeds by hurting human beings stretch us. Courageous achievements by handicapped people deepen our gratitude to the Father. Gestures of generosity by the poor challenge our use of money. Acceptance by others strengthens our acceptance of ourselves. Surprisingly, we can be impacted forever by a greeting from a stranger at a supermarket checkout counter, a casual remark by a neighbor, or a thoughtful message from an old acquaintance.

That is why ordinary people frequently have such extraordinary influence on our spiritual quest. Once a friend made me understand ethical pressures in modern business practices when he expressed his own frustration as we left a politically charged zoning hearing for a new church site: "Pastor, before we get this church built, this political system may make a cheat out of you." God reminded me through my friend that snow-white ethics are difficult to maintain in many business and political environments.

A little boy deepened my awareness of creation as he looked up from the Broadmoor Hotel pond near Colorado Springs to ask, "Mister, did you ever pet a duck like this?" The Father taught me through that charming, freckled-faced preschooler to marvel at the world around me.

A couple of years after my lifelong friend's wife died at 47, he helped me develop a new appreciation for marriage. I felt the depth of his loss when he said, "Dating at 50 is like taking on a second full-time job." Through my friend, God reminded me to cherish my own marriage more fully.

When we listen closely, our fellow human beings can be a challenging source of spiritual illumination whose words may ring in our hearts for months and years, perhaps a lifetime. Such enlightening messages often come from those who have no intention to influence us. Halford Luccock is right: "You find yourself in the exciting adventures of the mind opened to you by fine minds who awakened your mind, the riches of friendship given you by those who have walked with you, the sense of responsibility which has grown out of great tasks someone gave you to do, and the lift of ideas given you by someone who held them high before you."[10] God uses others to touch us with insight and inspiration, so that we become a living mosaic of everyone we have known.

God frequently uses people as mirrors to reflect how we look to Him and others. Psychiatrist Carl Jung underscores a principle of life that "we meet ourselves time and again in a thousand disguises of life."[11] Oswald Chambers, the devotional writer, affirms a similar idea in this wide-awake way, "Our heavenly Father has an amazing sense of humor. He will bring across your path the kind of people who show you what you have been to Him."[12] To accurately receive such data requires an intentional eagerness to understand the messages God is sending through others.

Nearly every relationship stretches our spiritual development in some way. Some associations require strength we would never develop without the demanding expectations of others. As the child trusts the parent, the adult is forced to grow because he feels unworthy of such confidence. When a patient places wholehearted confidence in the physician, the conscientious doctor wonders how to measure up. When a dying saint puts full faith in the minister's words of hope, the pastor feels obligated to move beyond his own inner dryness. And some students stand on tiptoe to be all they can be when their teacher expects them to do well. A friend of mine tells about a little fellow who did so poorly in second grade that he was assigned to a new teacher. After a few weeks, his mother questioned his amazing improvement. The boy replied, "My teacher thought I was good, so I was." The hymn writer had the same idea when he sang, "I would be true, for there are those who trust me" (Howard Arnold Walter).

The Master Potter uses soul friends to form Christlikeness in us. This type of friend is more than an accommodating neighbor who cares for my mail when I leave town. A soul friend is more than an acquaintance who knew me before I started school, met me as a mixed-up college student, or lived down the street in Carmichael, Calif. A lot more is involved than my childhood playmates on French Road near Detroit's city airport, parents of my children's friends in Moses Lake, or fellow graduate students of Vanderbilt.

By soul friends, I mean those with whom I maintain a relationship of depth that is quickly revived with only a few sentences after we have been apart for months or years.

Cherish Relationships / 147

Such a bond started with a significant "aha" moment when they made a never-to-be-forgotten contribution to my life. From some small beginning, a trust grew between us, so that they accept me just as I am, even though they may not fully understand me. These friends provide guidance and support to help me find deeper significance in my journey of faith; they are Christian through and through. This relationship is not better than family ties—just different.

Let me introduce several soul friends who help connect the fragments of living into a meaningful whole for me. AFH, old enough to be my father but at one time my editor in chief, always encouraged me to write, but he made an enduring investment in our friendship when he walked with me to a tiny new grave near Kansas City where we buried my first son, who died a little while before birth. AJW, VH, MH—three women with hotlines to heaven have taken my desperate needs to the Father's throne and returned with incredible life-changing answers. ESM, gentle spirit and decent human being, my superior and colleague in an important Christian assignment, trusted me so implicitly that I became the person he thought I was. BMS, my absolutely loyal friend for 25 years, is embarrassingly extravagant with confidence and affirmation. BB, now with the Father, believed in my dream based on an idealism that probably should have corroded long ago. MAL, my publishing friend for 30 years, helped me build several dreams into realities that impacted hundreds of ministers and brought enormous fulfillment. KD, woman of startling creativity and devotion, first came into my life as a pastor to my college-age sons and now shares wonderful times of friendship with their parents. MJK, childhood buddy, adult friend, and faithful nurturer, packed two lifetimes as a soul friend into her less than 50 years.

My list of soul friends is too long to continue, but I am better and nobler because of them. With apology to the writer of the Hebrews Epistle, what more can I say? The world and I are not worthy of them. To be spiritually whole, everyone needs soul friends—someone with whom you can stretch, agonize, and grow. They are available all around us if we are willing to nurture them.

Then, too, when someone else cares, we pay closer attention to how we live. Helen Hayes describes this give-and-take: "We relish news of our heroes, forgetting that we are extraordinary to somebody, too."[13] Just to be aware that someone knows and prays empowers us to remember and live by what is significant and true. So husbands need wives to appreciate them as much as wives need their husbands' unconditional love. Employees grow when superiors expect greatness, but employers need subordinates to depend on them too. Churches need loving pastors, but ministers are most fulfilled when they serve affirming congregations. Relationships provide a stimulating two-way street, so that friends help each other grow.

Though every bud of friendship may not ripen into mature fruit, why not welcome each green shoot and enjoy every colorful blossom. The secret is to give and receive as much as possible from every relationship. Accept folk as they are, and allow them to determine the depth of their friendship with you. Be grateful for those who share a passing "good morning" on the street corner, cherish those who believe in your cause, and treasure friends of the years. Pay careful attention to each new friendship simply because long-term relationships always start out as casual acquaintances.

The deepest lessons of Christianity can never be learned in isolation. It is nearby neighbors, faithful friends, and even casual associates who create warmly affirming climates where spirituality thrives. Think of the possibilities. It happens when teenagers ask, Who am I? and Where am I going? In middle years, relationships provide reassuring support for mid-life crisis. And when old age approaches, faithful friendships affirm the meaning of life. Though human existence without friends feels like a dreary desert, fulfilling relationships add strength, vigor, and wisdom to life.

Family—a Powerful Growth Resource

Many contemporary families seem at war with God's plans for them. Divorce has so drastically changed society that traditional families like the TV Waltons seem to be gone forever. And because 50 percent of mothers of children under 18 now work outside their homes, their offspring are able to have more of what they want and less of what they need.

Family alienation has deepened due to vanishing moral and social values; illegitimacy, desertions, promiscuity, divorce, and juvenile crime make the situation even more alarming. There is an increasing awareness of old problems like violence, abuse, drugs, and codependency that make families dysfunctional. This tidal wave of family disintegration causes despair for individuals and unnumbered problems for society. Recently a grown man told me with a painful sigh that multiple divorces made his family tree look as if it had been hit by lightning. All of this increasing sense of loss frustrates the whole of society even as a new generation is being raised in jeopardy.

Not to oversimplify or unduly complicate the issues, brokenness appears to be the major problem. It is the brokenness of a family who gives up the struggle to stay together due to drunkenness. It is the brokenness of emotional abuse that limits a child's learning and keeps the parents from finding fulfillment in their marriage and family. It is the brokenhearted four-year-old boy in divorce court who must tell his father good-bye until a visit can be arranged at the whim of his alienated parents. These fractured relationships emphasize the fact that few things are worse than a house that has ceased being a home.

In light of such devastation, is it time to seriously consider the biblical solution of forgiveness and reconciliation?

Could it be that the situation is desperate enough that we are ready to move toward family solidarity and move away from selfishness, which satisfies no one? Are we ready to give up egotism for tenderness? Can we find ways to rebuild loving harmony into our families? Since the immoral drumbeat of broken commitments and secularization of society has brought us to this brink of despair, is it now possible to follow God's call back to sanity, survival, and even satisfaction?

Though centuries old, the remedies offered by spirituality hold powerfully potent cures for this destructive epidemic. Like fine china, a family is beautiful to experience but easy to mar or break. To paraphrase the Peace Corps slogan, building a family may be the toughest job you will ever love. But spiritual resources, when seriously applied to life, can help married couples discover that renewed affection can be better than new love. Parents can discover again that children can be enjoyed rather than endured. Family links are worth constant nurturing because they affect everything today, even as they cast a long influence across future generations.

But bloodlines do not automatically provide a feeling of belonging or sense of family. Neither do biological connections guarantee a mosquito-free picnic of lifelong family happiness. Rather, a real family—biological or adoptive—demands hard work to nourish caring interactions that stimulate the mind, comfort the soul, and shelter the body.

Though parents hold a child's hand for only a few years, their imprint on his heart lasts forever. And though children may live in the home for only 18 or 20 years, their effect on parents is unforgettable. Peter DeVries' idea is true, "The value of marriage is not that adults produce children, but that children produce adults."[14] This two-way influence between parents and children is more incredible than any family trait originating from genes or chromosomes.

Think of the adventure. Kathy Coffey's essay "With Baby and Briefcase" describes a coworker's question,

"How can you work all day, then go home to your kids?" Though the questioner expected a discouraging litany, she answered, "I couldn't work without them."[15] Then she tells how benefits outweigh exhaustion when her kids shout, "Mom, you look beautiful today." Then, too, she feels richly rewarded as they wait by the walk to show her the first yellow crocuses of spring. Parenting pays special rewards, even though it is tough, tiring, hard work.

Having children gives us the perfect excuse to enjoy the soul-satisfying feeling of being a child again—to laugh, to cry, to grow, to learn, and to depend. Maybe God looks on the whole human race and says, "I love children. I want to help children. It doesn't matter if they are 8, 28, or 88. They are not brittle, and they take risks." There is something spiritually stimulating to cultivate childlike trust, curiosity, and affection toward the Father.

Relationships between children in a family also offers potential for growth and strength. Brothers and sisters must work to be friends; this need is graphically explained in a letter printed in an Ann Landers column from Lucille of St. Louis to her sons: "Nobody else will remember the Christmases you had, the tree house you built, the day you learned to ride a bike, the fun you had trick or treating, the teacher you loved in the third grade and the kittens born in the laundry room. There will be only the two of you and you had better love each other now, because 60 years from now only you will remember all the wonderful experiences you shared and those memories will be golden."[16] Such a common heritage of shared experiences provides the foundation for siblings to become best friends. To experience inner wellness, everyone needs someone like a brother or sister to increase self-acceptance, heal memories, and build abiding values into the fabric of life.

Extended families provide for companionship across generations too. Then elders can have a part in shaping new generations with the family roots they represent, even as the young, with their adventuresome risks, teach the elderly. Regardless of experience or age, persons learn a lot about inner wellness from two or more generations in their own families. These possibilities continue throughout the entire life span because today's children will likely become someone's parents, while these same people are forever tied to their parents and grandparents. Such relationships across generations should be nourished simply because everyone stands to receive so much benefit.

One grandfather, an influential churchman respected by thousands, said shortly after retirement, "Only one's family makes much difference when evening shadows start to fall." How sad, then, that so many approach mature years with little investment in happy family associations. A lonely career woman has sad firsthand knowledge of this problem because she spent inadequate effort in building relationships with her grown children, and, as a result, in her early 60s she said, "Now I know life is measured by family and not by finance." She suffered lonely alienation during old age because her discovery came too late to start over again. Yet some people wear emotional blinders that keep them from seeing this issue.

A father in his 50s whose sons, since high school, did not suit him with their appearance, life-styles, or career choices reasoned, "I'm ready to bury the hatchet. Whatever their rejection of my standards, they are my sons, and I want to be close for whatever time we have left." An adult friendship started the day he made that decision; his sons entered freely into the new friendship, accepting their father on a more equal basis with shared respect.

A grandmother, forced into second-generation parenting because of her daughter-in-law's death from a pulmonary embolism, shrugs off the acclaim she received by saying, "All I get is a lot of pleasure out of every happiness the grandchildren have."[17] How fortunate for all that grandchildren, grown son, and grandmother made life an adventure for each other.

In family life, because of constant change, there is always more building of relationships to be done. As childhood, parenthood, and grandparenthood fly by, life forces us to let go of some relationships so that we can take hold of others. Each adjustment has its rewards, even though another demand always waits around the next corner. Think of the joyous possibilities: I am a better person because these changing circumstances required me to learn to be a grown son, husband, son-in-law, father-in-law, and now a grandfather.

Love, acceptance, and commitment in families are as much needed for inner health as food is required for physical health. Walter Tubbs is right: "We are fully ourselves only in relation to each other."[18] Though everybody needs something like a family, many moderns may exist for a lifetime without experiencing the positive influences a real family offers. Consequently, even though earlier forms of family may be gone forever, rediscovery of the strengths they provide is needed now more than ever.

Everyone needs something like a family to nourish the spirit as much as he needs shelter against the sun, rain, and snow. Family trees flourish as they are rooted in affection and affirmation.

Church—a Family Such as Everyone Needs

A divorcée in her early 30s, drawn and wrinkled by dissipation, moved to a strange city with her young children. Though she longed to begin a new life, her past drove her to places where she formed dead-end relationships. One evening in a near-drunken state, her heart questioned her about the purpose of her existence. At nearly the same moment, a young neighbor couple appeared at her door to offer a cordial invitation to attend church with them the next morning, Sunday. Though she hesitated, their friendly persuasion was hard to resist.

True to the couple's promise, they came the next morning to take the mother and her little family to a small church not far from her house. As the tiny congregation offered her friendship, she felt drawn to Christ and surrendered the shreds of her broken life to the Savior. Along with her newfound faith, her sense of belonging increased as the people of God offered her unconditional love and overlooked her strange ways. Her new church friends provided such wholehearted support that she began calling them "the family I never had."

Such magnetism can be possessed by every church, an attractive alternative to family disintegration. Then, in its finest hour the church actually becomes the family of God. Then, whenever this family of faith gathers anywhere around the globe in small clusters or larger congregations, a weary wanderer finds a home and joins a company of prodigals at the Father's table to enjoy a homecoming feast together. With poetic insight, songwriter Byran Jeffery Leech rivets these reconciliation possibilities into our hearts:

We are God's people, the chosen of the Lord,
Born of His Spirit, established by His Word;
Our cornerstone is Christ alone,
   And strong in Him we stand.
O let us live transparently,
   And walk heart to heart and hand in hand.*

A friendly word like *church*, backed by traditions of 2,000 years frequently blundering and sometimes bordering on the barbaric, creates many mental images in conversation, print, or sermon. For some, the word conjures up an arid meetinghouse where institutional preservation reigns supreme. It may trigger memories of joyous weddings or sad funerals. For others, the mere mention of the word *church* produces mental pictures of edifices as diverse as the Cathedral of Notre Dame or the little church in the wild-

---
*© Copyright 1976 by Fred Bock Music Co. All rights reserved. Used by permission.

wood. Some automatically translate the word to mean Pastor Brown's church. Church, for others, means a literal sanctuary—a safe space for withdrawal from life. For a frightened few, it may be a stronghold against change.

In its fullest meaning, however, the church is a joyous rendezvous of spiritual discovery with serious pilgrims built on a frank admission that going it alone usually means going nowhere in spiritual development. But going together leads us to the Giver of harmony, who heals destructive memories and painful emotions. Like a glorious family reunion, this going together encourages us to become all we can be.

These meaningful associations resource the authentic church, so that it channels the efforts of ordinary people into life-changing exploits. Its worship and proclamation refresh the God-seeker's soul with an expanding vision of Christlikeness. Contact with the people of God produces hope and gives us a sense of personal worth. The most important of all tests for the church is the difference it makes in the daily events of its members.

People are searching for a place of belonging because fast-lane living never satisfies in an ultimate sense. Consequently, a real church can never allow itself to become a Peyton Place of gossip nor provide a platform for destructive behavior worse than would be acceptable in a secular club; a quarreling, bitter church cannot speak to the world about anything. Rather, the church must foster a relational richness where all kinds of people gather to cherish each other, to discover meaning for life, and to seek God's will. That is what every church can be, a center of acceptance and love.

The church as a family of friends has the dual task of introducing people to divine resources and sensitizing them to human need. In many ways, it Christianizes believers at the same time it remedies secularism. In stimulating relationships, the church teaches that everything a human being possesses is a gift-loan from God to be used for an individual's good and to be available to others—a powerful prevention against greed. In this extended family, fellow believers are closer-than-blood brothers and sisters where being cherished supplies a health-giving antidote for isolation, loneliness, and tension.

Such a Christ-centered family, called the church, offers the instruction of an exciting school where learning is a joy, the healing of a supernatural hospital where inner health is assured, the resources of a rich bank where human needs are abundantly supplied, and an accepting home where love is supreme. As a network of happy friends, the church becomes a channel through which people strengthen each other in uniquely satisfying ways.

The church, by definition and essence, possesses latent power to be a restoring community of becomers. Vernon Grounds clarifies the issue: "On a human level, every New Testament church is to be a family, a fraternity, and a fellowship, whose members share profoundly and pervasively."[19] This means many facets of the inner world, like beliefs, aspirations, motives, emotions, and choice, are impacted by this radical association of love where persons struggle to be godly together. Consequently, these significant relationships test questionable practices and create a climate where everyone feels valued as a child of God. Inasmuch as this unique blending of divine and human resources cannot be found in other organizations, the church must be encouraged to become what it was intended to be.

Sadly, the church, planned by God to be a resource for spiritual growth, often spends too much energy perpetuating itself. As a result the stirring adventures of life together are numbed by secondary concerns like larger facilities, expanded programs, or fading traditions. In other equally frustrating situations, the church is sometimes reduced "to either a pep rally for Jesus or an irritating set of restrictions."[20] But an almost irresistible attraction emanates from an authentic New Testament church that is committed to caring for people in place of institutional maintenance. And the church's vigor increases in the process of giving itself to these lofty purposes.

The church, to be the Christ-centered family everyone needs, must resist Madison Avenue hype and induced enthusiasm for the higher good of obedient worship of God based on Holy Scripture and a vibrant fellowship with one another. Inasmuch as the real business of the church is people, cold orthodoxy, meaningless rituals (whether liturgical or evangelical), polished professionalism, complacent traditions, and self-centered use of ecclesiastical power must be forsaken.

The aim of our Lord was not to create a small, ingrown religious sect but to revolutionize the whole human enterprise. That means in place of lesser things, the Scripture must be taught with affectionate authority and true-to-life application. Public services must inspire commitment, worship, and praise. The resources of the gospel must be focused meaningfully on contemporary life as God's answers to the mind-boggling problems raging inside modern people. Stuffy forms must be infused with vitality to provide a safe place for self-disclosure, mutual trust, and an openness to the new things God wants to do. And lay and ministerial leaders must together become willing servants of all.

The church, much more than a mere commercial enterprise, is intended by God to be a family of seekers whose reason for being is to help everyone discover supernatural resources for inner wellness. This dormant capability of the local church must be activated to restore troubled people to purposeful living and lead them into wholeness. The main problem facing the church, then, is to apply its unique resources to the needs of ordinary people.

Because such resourceful relationships *can* be developed, they *must* be developed. Then empty churches will be full again. Then faith living will be fun. Then saints will salt society in factories, governments, corporations, and everywhere else. Confused secularists will experience transformation. Then the Bible will be respected again as the Authority for living. Preachers will be reenergized. Once again sin will be forgiven and forsaken. Then brokenness will be healed, and peace will reign. Exposure to and participation in these realities of spirituality will end the famine of faith as congregations, families, and individuals pray and sing together again.

The obvious question is, Where can such a church be found? This query must be seriously considered because it implies that such churches do not exist or that the standard is unreachable. The most effective answer starts with a hearty effort to improve the church where you attend; begin by infusing every relationship in that church with the love of Christ. This process develops rapidly when each person begins to feel how deeply he is valued.

It is a fact of this life together that receiving love enhances the ability to give love, thereby creating a supportive circle of enabling relationships. In such an environment, it becomes almost automatic for people to return affirmation for affirmation, encouragement for encouragement, and affection for affection. Every believer, regardless of talent or training, is called and resourced by God to build these kinds of associations with other Christians. As we meet together in such a fellowship of faith, we enjoy the privilege of saying warm words and doing helpful deeds to stimulate others to a deeper appreciation of the gospel, to stronger commitment of servanthood, and to lasting friendships centered in our common love for Christ.

Why not do your part to transform your church into a loving family of God? The fine art of growing such a spiritual family helps people find joy, conviction, and energy in their relationship to Christ and their commitment to each other. This effort makes real the motto of a Colorado church, "Love grows here."

How to Build Spirituality Through Relationships

One of the false fantasies of life, fed by unrealistic expectations, makes us believe someone will soon begin loving us and start a satisfying friendship with us. But because such a wait may be disappointingly long, why not take the lead by reaching out to someone else? It may be easier to begin than to wait. The time is now, and here are some suggestions on how to begin.

1. Cherish People as Spokespersons for God. See every person you meet as a God-given source of inspiration and information, always available to you. View folks as personal spiritual growth inspirers. Value every human being as a significant messenger from God to draw you closer to Him. Listen carefully to what they tell you. Give special attention to the young and the elderly.

2. Cultivate Growth Friendships. An unidentified veteran of the way offers this wise counsel: "If you want to know God better, keep company with His best friends." Seek out spiritually strong people as a source of inner development. We all know and care for people who deplete our spiritual and emotional energies. But for spiritual growth, your repertoire of friends must also include strengtheners who stimulate faith and bring encouragement into your life. Intentionally build associations with those who will be honest in their evaluation of you and will hold you accountable for your commitments to spiritual growth. Apply this Japanese proverb to your personal spiritual development: "When the character of a man is not clear to you, look at his friends." Stay close to spiritually strong people.

3. Use Criticism to Evaluate Your Motives. Though critics are seldom comforting, they may be partially right. Their discontent often contains small degrees of useful information you can use in self-evaluation. Mistakenly, many reject a critic's opinions before checking their inner world to see if these criticisms contain even a small amount of needed correction. However, when we accept criticism as partially accurate or partially deserved, it shapes our thinking and molds our character. Maybe Abba John, one of the early desert fathers, helps when he advises us to give up heavy burdens and take on a light burden; then he explains, "The heavy burden is judging other people, the light burden is accepting the judgments of others."[21] Critics can help us deepen our spiritual development.

4. Accept People as You Find Them. Though most people are wonderful, Jesus has had a few weird friends in every generation, and He still does. To welcome someone into your life does not mean you endorse all his actions, nor does it require responsibility on your part to change him.

Often valuable new perspectives come from unexpected sources. A New York City street person may have an insight that an ivory tower scholar needs to hear. A new convert imprisoned on death row has something vital to say to believers who came to Christ in childhood. The old have wisdom to share with the young even as novice Christians and veteran saints have profound insights for each other. Ted Engstrom offers sound advice: "Would we not live wiser, happier, and more fulfilled lives if we enjoyed each other for what the other person is? Young or old, black or white, rich or poor, adult or child."[22] Such interactions sharpen our own spiritual development.

Why not value everyone's uniqueness? Cherish folks simply because God created them with such infinite variety. Allow them to be who they are, and catch a glimpse of what they can become by grace. You need never lose the excitement their uniqueness offers because every person will be different each time you meet. Try to live the advice of the old Shaker manuscript of 1848, "Open the windows and doors and receive whomever is sent."

5. Write a Relationship Journal. Using any form of writing you wish, list three affirming and three difficult relationships in your present circle of friends and family. Simply write your feelings about your experiences with these six people; then lay each summary aside for several days before you evaluate them. Later when you read them again, you will be amazed to see how your diary provides a spiritual autobiographical sketch of your own life. Though these summaries help you sort out what you see in family and friends, they also provide a mirror to help you see yourself. Such self-awareness is the first step in self-mastery.

6. Invest Love in Your Church. Though many present-day churches are infected by a sterile rationalism or a bleak sense of duty, one person sharing agape love can transform any situation quickly. From a survey of 8,600 people, the Institute of American Church Growth of Pasadena, Calif., found that "loving churches attract more people, regardless of their theology, denomination, or location." In the same report, church growth specialist Win Arn added, "Love can be taught—and learned—in churches that seem to have forgotten how."[23] In a loving church fellowship, everyone gains support and satisfaction, including visitors, newcomers, members, and leaders. This miracle of caring relationships takes its pattern and power from Jesus.

7. Renew Family Commitments. A loving family is among life's richest blessings. Apply that beautiful word *family* to all primary relationships, including spouse, children, parents, grandparents, siblings, cousins, aunts, and uncles. And should your biological family be nonexistent or broken, develop other support groups to serve as a substitute family.

Of all the gifts you give to your family, none is as precious as the gift of yourself. Open a line of emotional credit for every member of your real or adopted family where you become the cosigner, signifying that you will always be available. Then go out of your way to be helpful, to be supportive, and to listen. This simple practice will work wonders because love grows with expression just as commitment expands with practice. Being a loving spouse and a supportive parent are the most important jobs anyone ever had—and the most satisfying too. At the same time every family, whether biological or adopted, is a God-given fortress to protect you against stress.

Someone in your family connection needs tenderness now. Fascinating starting points could be near-kin, like rebellious teenagers, grown children, or aging parents. You can lower your own stress by doing a loving deed for someone who needs to know you are thinking of him; a phone call, written note, or greeting card is a good way to start. Give your family reason to know your support is dependable and lasting. Speak caring words they understand and appreciate. Try praising them to strength. Let them know you admire them as friends and that your commitment goes beyond biological connections. Try going beyond the call of duty in giving, loving, and serving.

8. Restore Broken Relationships. Inasmuch as love and forgiveness always start as intentional acts, set your will to nurture relationships at home, at work, and in the world. Even though we may not be able to completely control our feelings, we can strengthen sandpapered relationships with Christ-motivated thoughts and deeds.

Avoid anger and retaliation. Forgive quickly like Lincoln, whose heart had "no room for the memory of a wrong." Enrich each person you meet with a word of encouragement or an act of kindness. Rejoice in another person's good fortune as quickly as you would sympathize with his pain or sorrow. Make strengthening an object of your conversation, and remember that a two-minute discussion of someone's faults can destroy a lifelong friendship.

When an unfortunate attitude or unkind action fractures a relationship, take the first step toward reconciliation. Your action builds a bridge the other person can use to walk back into your heart.

9. Give a Gift of Presence. Friends ill in body, battered in spirit, or disappointed by life do not need more words; but a gentle presence and a listening ear are always welcomed. Giving time and careful listening are among the most precious gifts anyone ever gives to another person. This gift of presence turns out to be a wonderful adventure because the giver usually receives more than he gives. Never cease cherishing people, and force your lips to tell them when your heart feels love and affirmation for them.

10. Tackle Relational Frontiers. Like Columbus in search of new worlds, think of yourself as an explorer who builds rich relationships. Consider broken people as prime candidates for friendship, reconciliation, and rehabilitation. Encourage loving interaction in your church. Count your family, regardless of size or closeness, as a center for spiritual development. Friendships, church fellowship, and family are God's solutions to isolation. Try to turn your loneliness into opportunities for developing satisfying friendships. View distance and mobility as challenges rather than barriers to maintaining friendships; the phone and mail can help you succeed.

Relationships really matter when life is reduced to basics. Everyone needs to love and to be loved. People are usually wonderful, sometimes strange, and always interesting.

> "Prayer in the sense of petition, asking for things, is a small part of it; confession and penitence are its threshold, adoration its sanctuary, the presence and vision and enjoyment of God its bread and wine. In it God shows himself to us."
> —C. S. Lewis

9
PRAY CHANGE INTO YOUR LIFE

Tests terrorize students, and this exam was no exception. In response to the question "Identify and discuss five kinds of prayer," the professor expected members of the class to answer "adoration, confession, petition, thanksgiving, and intercession." Imagine the instructor's surprise when a mischievous student wrote two exams, one for himself with correct answers and a second test paper for a fictitious character named Willy Lump-Lump. Though the significance of Willy's name still mystifies me, his preposterous answers—oral, silent, standing, sitting, and bedtime—sound as vague and humdrum as much current thinking about prayer.

While God intends prayer to tame stress, moderns frequently intensify their tensions with muddled notions about divine-human communication. Other misconceptions confuse those who pray or create guilt for those who don't. The issues are perplexing: Does it matter if I pray? Is someone listening? What about unanswered prayer?

Before one prays, must all questions be answered? No. Unanswered ambiguities surround us on many levels of the human experience. Though few people understand the intricacies of medicine, mathematics, or electricity, everyone enjoys the benefits. And travelers keep flying, though few know much about aerodynamics.

Is it not enough to call witnesses into life's courtroom to attest that prayer works? Ordinary folks and devout saints from every generation in human history vouch for the validity of prayer; it has reduced stress for millions across centuries. And it still does.

Though the dynamics and definitions may not be fully understood, prayer impacts life on significantly substantial levels. The towering possibilities show in the answer the college professor expected on that long-ago exam.

Adoration, as a prayer of reverent wonder, lifts an individual to an attitude of worship and reminds him of who God is and what He does. Defined as "reverent appreciation raised to its loftiest terms,"[1] adoration forms the foundation for all other types of praying. It creates awareness of God's nearness in daily events and encourages a personal response of praise.

The Psalmist models adoration as he leads us in singing, "Bless the Lord, O my soul: and all that is within me, bless his holy name" (103:1, KJV). Adoration and worship, important components of wholeness, are found in abundant measure at the place of prayer.

Confession frees from damaging guilt as sin, omission, and stupidity are admitted to a loving Father. It includes the ancient statesman's cry for his nation's sins, "O my God, I am ashamed and blush to lift my face to thee, my God, for our iniquities have risen higher than our heads, and our guilt has mounted up to the heavens" (Ezra 9:6, RSV). It shines through the robust request Jesus made to His Father in the model prayer, "Forgive us our debts, as we also have forgiven our debtors" (Matt. 6:12). Confession, without self-earned deservings, makes us appreciative recipients of God's forgiveness.

Petition, the most prevalent of all prayer forms, expresses urgent desire. Considered the most elementary level of prayer, petition openly seeks divine aid in the midst of human powerlessness and the crushing weight of the unknown. This kind of prayer deals with the whole range of human need, including heartfelt pleas for daily bread, deliverance from temptation, and the coming of the Kingdom. Everyone prays at this level at one time or another.

Thanksgiving relieves stress because it draws attention away from self-centered requests to blessings we have already received. When one expresses gratitude for shelter, he is not likely to be asking God for a bigger house. When an individual praises God for a loving family, he does not complain about high grocery bills. When a person rejoices over the memory of his deceased loved one's well-lived life, grief about death's separation is lessened. The grateful pilgrim prays, "O Lord my God, I will give thanks unto thee for ever" (Ps. 30:12, KJV). Gratitude cures envy and self-pity, high producers of stress.

Intercession, a soul cry to God for another, longs for others to find peace of heart, healing for soul and body, or victory over a debilitating enslavement. This aggressive kind of praying kindles faith for both intercessor and receiver. As an advocate for another, the person who intercedes becomes a victorious though struggling warrior in a taxing battle against sin, evil, and darkness. This type of prayer wants all to be completely aware and freed from the false claims of technology, sophistication, and prosperity.

Intercession, tough work with revolutionary impact beyond our knowing, increases the spiritual stamina of the one who prays, even though the prime concern of intercession may be individuals, groups, or even the world. Writer Jane Edwards rightly insists: "Intercessory prayer is not a substitute for action. It is an action for which there is no substitute."[2] The New Testament Church strikingly illustrated effective intercession when that small band of believers prayed Peter out of prison (Acts 12:5 ff.). And Christian history, from the Early Church until now, records examples of intercessors whose prayers reformed people, transformed circumstances, and revolutionized nations. Intercession makes a pivotal difference in both our inner and outer worlds.

Each of these prayer patterns alleviates stress, sometimes defined as deadness toward God. This astonishing power prayer has over tension is explained by Alexis Carrel, the medical researcher: "The results of prayer can be measured in terms of increased physical buoyancy, intellectual vigor, moral stamina, and understanding of the realities underlying physical relationships. How does prayer fortify us with such dynamic power? When we pray, we link ourselves with the inexhaustible power that spins the universe. We ask that a part of His power be apportioned to our needs. Even in asking, our human deficiencies are filled, and we arise strengthened and repaired."[3] Stress begins to disappear as we pray, and we find liberating freedom from overattention to patterns and forms of prayer in Augustine's advice, "We come to God by love and not by navigation."[4] Our yearnings for inner unity, wholeness, and hope compel us to pray. And God answers.

How Does Prayer Change Those Who Pray?

Apparently a "no meaning" malaise hammerlocks much of our contemporary thought and feeling. This growing dissatisfaction—a kind of cynical boredom about money and respectability—means many moderns think something is missing or wrong. Compelling evidence shows up in the evening TV news, recent novels, morning papers, political rhetoric, and casual conversation at the corner bar among "good ol' boys." But prayer, as an act of faith, dares us to believe that the wrongs can be righted and the missing essentials can be found through the petitions of ordinary folks like us. One writer's comment makes the issue crystal clear: "Prayer is dangerous business. You could wind up being changed."

Less obvious, but at least as important, multitudes of people believe prayer changes situations and other people, but they never think about how it affects them. But it changes them; a life of prayer involves us in continuous remolding by the Master Potter. No one prays for another without some change coming over him; the change may be in our viewpoint about those for whom we pray, some deeper sympathy, some stronger sense of worth, or some new delight in our own character development.

• **Prayer unchains an individual from old habits of feeling, thinking, and acting.** Having one's inner eyes opened as a result of prayer may at first feel uncomfortable because "we want to be left alone with our loyalties, with our good sense, and with the ways we understand."[5] Nevertheless, genuine prayer—an inner attentiveness to God's voice—kindles surprising insights, corrects false assumptions, questions comforting distortions, and destroys flattering myths we believe about ourselves. This clarification shows us what to look for so that we see the big picture of God's purpose in the world and in us.

• **Prayer takes us on a voyage of inner discovery.** Like seeing through a microscope, a person sometimes sees closeup, minute details during prayer, while on other occasions prayer is more like looking through binoculars, where distant objects are brought into clearer view. Conversations with the Father focus the soul's sight, so that we see things as they look to God. Then, in heart-to-heart dialogue with God, we discover a new life to live, a new servanthood to serve, and a new destiny to fulfill. Thus prayer is absolutely necessary for those who wish to make sense of the worlds within, without, and beyond.

• **Prayer shapes us into Christlikeness.** Christlikeness is the highest human pursuit; it has always been and still is. The process of becoming like our Lord begins as we open ourselves to God in trust so that He can restore us into what He intended when He first created us. Then we are brought face-to-face with the essential elements of wholeness and with ways to develop them. This underrecognized, almost latent, potential of prayer to shape us into Christlikeness shines through S. D. Gordon's summary of Jesus' communication with the Father: "When perplexed, Jesus prayed. When hard pressed by work, He prayed. When hungry for fellowship, He prayed. He chose His associates and received His messages upon His knees. If tempted, He prayed. If criticized, He prayed. If fatigued in body or weary in spirit, He had recourse to His one unfailing habit of prayer."[6] All these Christ-shaping ingredients of prayer stymie our stress. Consequently, the ultimate outcome of lifelong conversation with God is not what we receive but what we become; the Christ-centered life we seek and find is a genuinely authentic quality life.

God sometimes sends jolting surprises during prayer—some that affirm and some that discipline. Then, honest communication with the Father forces an egotist to admit his absolute dependence on God, so that tensions originating from his self-directed achievements vanish. When the proud person prays, he is reminded that without God there is no food, sun, or oxygen; that shatters his arrogance. When the capable though overly dependent believer prays, the Father sometimes answers, "Get up and go answer your own prayer." Those who intercede for world evangelization sometimes hear an astonishing command, "Give of thy sons to bear the message glorious; / Give of thy wealth to speed them on their way" (Mary Ann Thomson). When impulsive folks pray, they often receive a "not yet" answer. And those who come to God with sniffling self-pity sometimes experience deafening silence, indicating how preposterous their complaints sound to God.

Every untarnished, selfless prayer changes the pilgrim for the better. The Christlike possibilities that flow to an authentic life of devotion shaped by prayer are summarized by Muggeridge: "To sacrifice rather than grab, to love rather than lust, to give rather than take, to pursue truth rather than promote lies, and to humble oneself rather than inflate the ego."[7] The act of praying makes the petitioner nobler and humbler, a significant answer in itself to prayer.

- **Prayer requires wholehearted honesty.** Deception and hocus-pocus in the name of religion are common these days. Scripture, however, is brutally frank about honesty and purity: "Surely the arm of the Lord is not too short to save, nor his ear too dull to hear. But your iniquities have separated you from your God; your sins have hidden his face from you, *so that he will not hear*" (Isa. 59:1-2, italics added). This passage means unworthy thoughts and sinful deeds hinder communication with God; He is interested in humility and authenticity. Every intention is accurately known to the Father; He looks beneath the masks we show each other to evaluate every attitude and action for its precise motivation. So God is not fooled by bad tempers and bluffing sins; they have to go if we desire closeness with Him.

Self-delusion, a cause of unrelenting stress, is often challenged during prayer. New resources at the place of prayer help us break out of self-made prisons of rationalizations and half-truths. In quiet, life-changing ways, communication with God questions unfounded prejudices and cross-examines strange notions that follow us into our quiet times. And prayer in strange, demanding ways pries into our petty bitterness and judges unresolved resentments we seem reluctant to confess.

- **Prayer judges integrity.** Unworthy motives and questionable actions cause a blush during prayer. But high-sounding dishonesty and evasive morality have become so common that they are hardly recognized or questioned. As a result, an educator teaches shoddily during the week but sings in the choir on Sunday. A Realtor gouges poor people on Saturday but teaches a Bible class on Tuesday. A published religious author takes time from his writing to divorce the wife of his youth to marry a woman half his age. A television evangelist, after confessing sexual sins, complains on the front pages of the newspapers because he is not allowed to return to a so-called ministry that lined his pockets with the sacrificial contributions of millions of viewers. This double-dealing even shows up in an auto repair shop when a mechanic gyps a widow on Wednesday after serving as a pious usher in the Sunday services. Additional examples are not hard to find.

This integrity issue, however, must be scrutinized even closer to home, inasmuch as every public evasion of morality has a serious counterpart in private lives like ours. God, like a military general, uses the quiet place of prayer as a reviewing stand, where He examines our conduct and inspects our character. The Father shows us our real self during prayer, the way we look to Him. Because besetting sins wait like ravenous wolves outside the back door of everyone's will, Buttrick rightly insists, "We must live in purity, not offering God an infected arm for service."[8]

Sin always poisons the reservoirs of the inner world. The Bible, candidly true to human experience, teaches that moral failures can never be completely hidden: "You may be sure that your sin will find you out" (Num. 32:23). While this teaching means others will eventually know about our sins, it also underscores the fact that wrongs keep tracking us down to ruin our self-worth and happiness.

Prayer shatters lurking illusions that fool us into believing that what we want is right. Better yet, it breaks down self-deception and pretense as it monitors our temperament and conversations. Such accurate evaluations, when coupled with divine resources for life-changing improvement, revolutionize a person from the inside out. In this process, prayer starts restoring a person to what he would have been if he had not been blighted by greed, ambition, self-centeredness, and lust.

- **Prayer provides a long-range perspective of life.** Prayer helps us see what lasts and what is truly important; it makes it possible for us to sort through bewildering ambiguities and trifling irritations. When life seems flat, this new perception teaches us that it may be too soon to judge whether an event is a credit or debit in the ledger of life. Think how many enjoy a fulfilling life now who once experienced crushing disappointments, and consider how many who started with promise have plateaued or declined. Prayer helps us see that an apparent liability may be a disguised blessing.

This grace of the long view impacted Joseph of Old Testament fame when his brothers came begging for food while he served in a high governmental position in Egypt. His daring testimony reassures us even now, though he carried the hurt of their wicked betrayal in his heart for half a lifetime: "You meant evil against me; but God meant it for good" (Gen. 50:20, RSV). Since all the facts are not in, it is too soon to accurately judge any situation. In the long term, failure may be a blessing, while success can turn out to be a curse.

How confusing that all sounds until we realize that stress decreases when our Lord's finale is added to all our prayers, "Not my will, but thine, be done" (Luke 22:42, KJV); this prayer moves us away from guilty acquiescence to satisfying trust in the purpose and providence of God. Anyone who has walked in the way for any period of time knows that God uses such unswerving relinquishment to shape our future with His holy love and superior wisdom. The result is a better life than anyone could possibly design or construct for himself.

- **Prayer frees us from self-centeredness.** Selfishness, the most destructive issue in spiritual formation, now comes in sophisticated packages labeled individualism, secularism, or narcissism. Everyone, even the gifted or brilliant, knows how nauseating self-centeredness can be in himself and in others. An overemphasis on self is the essence of sin, regardless of fancy names or colorful banners; this part of the human situation has not changed since creation. But after self-sovereignty has created king-sized problems, prayer causes us to assess ourselves accurately and forces us to realize our utter dependence is on God. Thereby, we are delivered from sickening self-centeredness as prayer uncovers our selfishness—especially the subtle, entrenched varieties.

Human beings have always sought better self-understanding, a problem intensified by competing contradictory voices in contemporary life. Interestingly, self-understanding increases during prayer when God asks tough self-revelation questions like:

Why do you want a job promotion? What will you do with a pay increase? Why do you want more financial security? How will your new authority be used? How will it affect your faith? How will this desired position impact significant people like your family?

Why do you pray for better health? How will you use it? Will your world, church, and family be better? Who will get the credit?

Why do you request that your spiritual life flourish? Will your actions show more integrity? Will anyone gain from your piety? Will you mirror the purposes of God more clearly?

Why do you pray for safety? Is it to avoid pain, humiliation, or discomfort? Will your personal security mean God is better served? Is anyone else helped because you are sheltered from disease or accident?

• **Prayer motivates action.** God makes assignments during prayer with considerably more regularity than any human teacher ever did. Thus, a disciple who intercedes for reconciliation between friends may be given a peace plan to initiate himself. While praying for a hurting neighbor, God may ask the petitioner, "What will you do?" And when an individual prays about his marriage, the Father may suggest ways to be a better mate.

Quiet, reflective prayer opens our hearts, so that we see ways to help answer our own petitions. Though the idea sounds revolutionary, it could be that God expects specific usefulness from us for every answered prayer.

Prayer without action is shadowboxing or self-deception.[9] This action side of prayer made a Civil War slave observe: "My prayer for freedom was never answered until it got into my heels and made me run away to freedom." The place where we bend our knee is only the port of call, but the open sea of usefulness lies beyond in sweaty, satisfying service.

Though we may feel inadequate in God's presence, a conversation with Him often energizes heroic action. Prayer links us with Omnipotence, so that the Helper's strength becomes our own.

This action-linkage component of prayer remedies the frustrating bane of a purposeless life. Sydney Harris, the columnist, accurately commented, "Few men ever drop dead from overwork, but many quietly curl up and die from undersatisfaction."[10] These days, thousands consider their jobs unimportant in terms of human or spiritual values. And lots of elderly folks believe they are no longer needed by family, society, or church. But when we pray, regardless of our age, experience, or vocation, Christ helps us make a telling difference in someone's life. Real prayer tears down feelings of uselessness.

No one can do anything more important than pray for another person. Frank Laubach explains how the hard work of intercession makes a difference in at least two lives: "Prayer is twice blest; it blesses him who gives and him who receives."[11] Then fulfillment and action flow together to enable us to change our world for Christ.

Though prayer is a useful service in itself, it also triggers life-changing action by the person who prays and in the person who is prayed for. The converse is true, too; every expression of Christian service without prayer is a terrible danger—a temptation to the ego of the doer and, therefore, a potential problem for the one who receives the benefit.

- **Prayer encourages plain talk with God.** Few conversations allow one to candidly express bewildering doubt and stressful frustration. But a person can say anything to God. In this dialogue, maddening confusion or appropriate rage can be expressed, like our Lord's tough question at the Cross, "Why hast thou forsaken me?" (Matt. 27:46; Mark 15:34, KJV).

Even though anguish is never evenly distributed throughout the human family, every person has heartaches. To pretend hurts do not exist only increases stress, but liberation begins when we speak frankly with God about our problems. Then our stress level goes down as God deals with our resentments, self-pity, and vulnerability.

Who has not been wounded by another's gossip or greed? Who has not suffered emotional trauma from someone's deception? Since we all have had our lives complicated by others, God is never shocked, threatened, or scandalized by anything we say to Him. Everyone needs a forum for such plain speaking.

- **Prayer admits absolute dependence.** People have always prayed in dark valleys, and they always will. During emergencies petitions automatically well up in the inner world. Even in the inner life of proud doubters, prayer seems to wait to be used at some underground gate. This irrepressible inner spring runs so deep that it cannot be dammed up by intellectual sophistication or class barriers. To borrow Fosdick's idea, "The reason we pray is simply that we cannot help praying."[12]

Demanding duties also press us to pray. Lincoln freely admitted during the most emotionally draining days of his presidency, "I have been driven to my knees by the overwhelming conviction that I had no other place to go; my own wisdom and that of those around me seemed insufficient for the day."[13] Less-known persons, like us, have similar feelings of inadequacies. Examples surround us. Without prayer, who really knows how to deal with marriage, parenting, divorce, reconciliation, forgiveness, or death? No one outgrows the necessity to pray; a homesickness for God always remains in the human heart regardless of attainment, social standing, or education.

As the naturalness of prayer is allowed into daily circumstances, it always lowers stress. This clearly shows in Luther's comparison of the divine-human dialogue with our physical pulse: "You cannot find a Christian man who does not pray; just as you cannot find a living man without a pulse beat that never stands still, but beats and beats on continually of itself, although the man may sleep or do anything else, so being all unconscious of this pulse."[14] This leads to the conclusion that prayer is as necessary to inner wholeness as the circulatory system is to physical health. No one can live very well for very long without praying.

Nearly everyone knows prayer becomes almost automatic in times of frightening danger and during the demands of crushing responsibilities. But why is prayer not used in more ordinary circumstances? Why limit such an incredible force to spasmodic use for extricating us from tight situations? Why not apply prayer to all of life instead of saving it as a last resort? This extraordinary power is also available on routine days. Those who pray in good weather know how to reach the Father during the storms.

• **Prayer cultivates friendship with God.** Dialogical prayer—an oasis of peace in a stress-filled world—opens new ways to know God better. Though communication concepts bombard us in books and magazines, even an elementary awareness of the process helps us see that conversation deepens relationships. Just as dialogue heightens our understanding of the viewpoint of a friend or mate, prayer helps us grasp God's ways better.

Effective communication, both hearing and speaking, takes conscious effort to really listen and understand. But during casual conversation something wonderfully exhilarating happens when a life-changing idea flashes into our minds. This common experience forms the basis for a psychotherapy concept that says people already possess answers to their own problems deep down in their psyche that can only be discovered in conversation with an accepting listener. If merely verbalizing a problem can open our minds to possible solutions, think of the enormous possibilities prayer offers.

A similar occurrence sometimes take place in the classroom. About the time a student finishes asking a question and before the teacher utters a word, the student sometimes says, "Now I see." A unique factor is at work; the answer came because the student actively participated in the dialogical process. When such an "aha" moment occurs during prayer, the promise of Scripture is fulfilled, "Before they call I will answer" (Isa. 65:24).

Fénelon offered guidance three centuries ago for such encounters: "Tell God all that is in your heart, as one unloads one's heart, its pleasures and its pains, to a dear friend. Tell Him your troubles, that He may comfort you; tell Him your joys, that He may sober them; tell Him your longings, that He may purify them; tell Him your dislikes, that He may help you to conquer them; talk to Him of your temptations, that He may shield you from them; show Him the wounds of your heart, that He may heal them."[15] Such candid communication with the Father takes spirituality into all levels of life, so that everything, including the mundane and majestic, are impacted by our conversations with Him.

Every word has meaning when true friends meet. That is why real prayer, much more than a traditional religious exercise, is actually an expression of esteem and friendship. Brother Lawrence explains the way to achieve such closeness: "We should establish ourselves in a sense of God's presence by continually conversing with Him."[16]

Frequent contact deepens every association, especially our relationship with God.

Prayer, at its essence, means nothing more but nothing less than a satisfying friendship with God. Closeness makes the difference. Such intimacy with the Father is a thousand times more satisfying than a childish SOS for help from the middle of a frightening problem.

How Does God Answer Prayer?

Some believers, because of presumed unanswered prayer, have quietly shut their heart's door to communication with God. They have given up on prayer; the whole effort has gone dead for them. At least once they experienced what appeared to be divine inaction when answers were most needed. Then, at the very time when prayer seemed to fail them, they were baffled by the success stories others told. Everyone knows someone whose prayers are always answered: they never miss a plane or lose their luggage; they have money while others are forced into bankruptcy; they sleep in warm beds while others spend cold nights on the streets; and others testify to disease-free, charmed lives.

That may be why some sincerely question, Is it true that God answers prayer? And if the reply is yes, they ask, Do you mean *all* prayers?

Maxie Dunnam's distinction between unanswered prayers and ungranted petitions helps free us from disappointing emotional baggage on this issue.[17] That means there is a significant difference between giving us what we think we want rather than what is best. That is the reason God's loving providence often keeps Him from granting every request, though His dependable character requires that all petitions be answered. Other factors must also be considered, such as our limited knowledge, God's plan for an ordered universe, the wisdom of leaving complicated issues in His care, and relief that some requests are not granted. Though His responses may not be according to our choosing, His answers always fit one of four categories: *yes, no, wait,* and *you must be kidding.*

A *yes* answer, most to our liking, is easiest to receive and understand. Because few people pray as a kind of casual spiritual walk through the park, their eagerness for answers is serious, often desperate. Thus, a straightforward *yes* from God is welcomed with gratitude. Then as the Answerer answers, life gets better and thanks flood our inner world. When such a reply comes, it is a grand time to rejoice and sing, "This is the Lord's doing; it is marvellous in our eyes" (Ps. 118:23, KJV).

The *no* answer, though we may go about our regular activities, takes much more submission and relinquishment than an unqualified *yes.* In the waiting period, Longfellow's logic is hard to refute: "What discord should we bring into the universe if our prayers were all answered. Then we should govern the universe and not God."[18] Though we deny any desire to run the world, God gets lots of unsolicited advice from us. As a loving Father who knows best, He sometimes answers with a firm *no.*

In mysterious ways, *no* may be the kindest of all possible answers. Think of the little mother's request, "Grant that one of these two sons of mine may sit at your right and the other at your left in your kingdom" (Matt. 20:21). Our Lord's *no* kept her sons from bitter heartbreaks that inevitably followed, even as they were saved from the shackles of their own power-crazed ambitions. God sometimes uses a *no* answer to protect us against an unwise request. At other times, *no* to a specific petition may turn out to be a powerful *yes* to our highest good.

Even Jesus received a *no* to His prayer in the Garden. And Paul was granted grace to endure his bothersome thorn following a *no* answer. These refusals did not harm Jesus or Paul because they met Someone at the place of prayer who empowered them to go on. The same thing happens to us. This sufficient enablement to deal with a *no* is often a much better answer than an unqualified *yes*.

A *wait* answer is among our most frustrating experiences because it requires passive trust when we want speedy action. In this day of instant gratification, moderns do not wait very well, but God's *wait* may be absolutely necessary because He sees ahead in His loving wisdom. Then again, delays may be required because some attitude or action is displeasingly wrong in us, an idea that scarcely occurs to anyone these days. James offers candid insight: "When you ask, you do not receive, because you ask with wrong motives, that you may spend what you get on your pleasures" (4:3). Perhaps the *wait* may sometimes mean conditions beyond our control are not yet right for a *yes* answer. Delay should not be taken to mean denial.

The issue of persistent prayer must be considered also. Could it be that God does not answer until a person is prepared to hold on? Could it be that perseverance makes us more ready for His answers? Perhaps persistence clarifies our motives, or maybe it helps us identify and overcome hindering difficulties like lesser loves, troublesome preoccupations, or selfish ambitions. Time spent in God's waiting room, often an important factor in our spiritual development, never means final refusal or ultimate rejection.

A fourth category, *you must be kidding*, must be considered. At first this answer shocks us, but it should not be considered to be a belittling insult. It could mean, do you realize what you are asking? It might mean, you are interceding about a settled issue in an orderly universe, such as gravity always works or thistles never produce roses. Or this answer may stem from requests where God has already acted, such as Jesus is Lord or sin always destroys.

This answer reminds us of God's faithfulness and the fact that some things are settled forever. No flippant putdown, this reply means that God is in control and reassures us that the Father has demonstrated His steadfast love throughout many yesterdays. This might be an encouraging answer to fretting folks who have experienced providential care all their days. This might even be the Father's assurance to the pitiful struggler who is afraid his requests will be denied. God answers *you must be kidding* to a variety of our misgivings.

Whatever the Father's response to our prayers, He is worthy of our worship because of who He is, not for what He does. The Answerer always answers—yes, no, wait, or you must be kidding. His answers heal stress just as surely as light dispels darkness.

How to Live a Life of Prayer

Most writers of the literature of spirituality agree that a daily tryst with God at a set time and specific place is highly desirable for inner-life health. We miss much when such a regular appointment is not kept with the Father because these special times provide such a splendid opportunity for God to help us make sense of life.

But there is another intensity of prayer, a ceaseless dialogue that puts the soul in continuous contact with God. Someone called it the Christ-saturated life. Far more than squeezing prayer into unused corners of human experience, this special way to live weaves prayer into the entire human drama. This life of unceasing prayer affirms Victor Hugo's wise sentence, "There are moments when, whatever be the attitude of the body, the soul is on its knees."[19] This minute-by-minute, day-by-day relationship puts us in touch with deep-rooted answers to vexing human questions.

Such a prayer-drenched life develops a vibrant faith and decreases the abstractions of religion. Scriptures for nourishing the life of prayer promise, "I am with you always, to the very end of the age" (Matt. 28:20), and "I am the vine; you are the branches" (John 15:5). Such a connected life provides enhanced fulfillment, harmonizes the inner and outer worlds, and even enables us to be more accepting and open to others. This prayer-immersed life makes us quit pretending to be omnipotent and infuses every activity with the Presence.

This perpetual practice of prayer may be described as in-Christ or Christ being formed in you. Calvin Miller uses the delightful term "Christifying," which he defines as "consciously viewing the people and circumstances in our lives with the eyes of Christ."[20] Paul had the same idea when he prayed for the Galatians, "I am again in travail until *Christ be formed in you!*" (4:19, RSV, italics added). While this continual devotion does not discount regular withdrawals with Deity, it takes spiritual resources into a dynamic flesh-and-blood encounter with life where we live it.

Exactly as these descriptions explain, this prayer-saturated life makes it possible for the Presence to bring meaning to the cutting edges of thought and achievement; it affects small details, wide horizons, nagging questions, gigantic dreams, and staggering obstacles. So in stride with God, this kind of fulfilled living laughs at Walpole's notion that our existence is "a comedy to those who think, and a tragedy to those who feel."[21] This in-Christness adds a noble quality to every phase of life.

At the same time, this life of prayer exposes the false promises of affluence, security, and conformity. It refutes arrogant pride and questions phony facades. This prayer-permeated kind of living empowers an individual to pursue needed action with courage. Continuous prayer lowers stress because it allows each sojourner to see the meaning of circumstances more clearly and to listen more intently to the messages God sends through so many sources.

This intense level of relationship enables us to pray: "Thank You, Father, for fulfilling my life as I worship with the people of God, as I enjoy a pleasant meal with family, as I converse with a neighbor, as I walk with an inquisitive child, as I listen to a challenging idea from an old friend, or as I receive love from my mate." Continuous conversation with the

Father makes us willing to trade fantasies of future greatness for the disciplines of present spiritual development.

In-Christness frees a pilgrim from living in the drab dreariness of a self-made world and infuses his experience with generosity, forgiveness, and faith. Its resiliency clobbers stress. This "Christifying" miraculously transforms thinking, feeling, and life-style, moving Christianity from vague notions to vital faith.

How to Pray Changes into Life

Locked into fixed prayer patterns, many overstressed people need new spiritual vigor. By definition, wholeness requires growth, which always necessitates change. Our task, therefore, is to overcome our natural reluctance to change and to unfamiliar patterns of prayer so that we can grow into what God calls us to become. The issue: How can creative changes be prayed into my life?

1. Pray Yourself Happy. While it is reassuringly true that intercessory prayer carries serious burdens close to its heart, the wonder of God's love generates gladness. Consequently, prayer must be more than a kind of reinforcement of fretting worries or a mulling of problems. Our petitions must move beyond gloomy desperation, which deals mostly with calamity or despair. The cornerstone for happy prayer is gratitude for simple blessings like shelter, air, water, health, and family.

A joyous conversation with the Father frees us to soar and sing, even as it breaks the chains of our failures and hurts. The Faithful One, who taught us laughter, stands beyond all our drab notions and weary anxieties. Take delight in God's goodness as you rejoice that prayer is neither black magic nor a blank check, but rather a celebration of a relationship with a Friend—Jesus Christ, our Lord.

2. Keep Alert to God's Surprises. There are many surprises along this holy way that often occur at amazing times. One writer tells about a little boy who, when urged to write his Christmas letter to Santa, kept procrastinating until his family wondered if he had caught on to their yule pretending. The boy finally revealed his reluctance: "If I write and tell Santa all the things I want, I'll never know what he just wanted to give me."[22] There is a pearl of wisdom in the child's thinking process: God has many intriguing surprises planned for every sojourner.

3. Take Prayer into the Details of Life. Never be content with superficial spirituality. One old spiritual veteran suggested that we pray about our praying. Push yourself to new depths of relationship with the Father as you open every corner of life to Him. Enter His presence with expectancy and respond fully to the assurance of His faithfulness.

One satisfying way to take prayer into the details of life is to form a mental picture of petitions already being answered, so that sick friends are seen as well and troubled marriages are viewed as being emotionally healed. Or, when asked a probing question or meeting a new friend, you may want to cultivate the practice of taking a five-second prayer break; simply pause for a five-second silent prayer, asking for wisdom and grace before you speak.

Another well-tested spiritual exercise begins and ends each day with prayer. By turning your first thoughts to God each morning, you provide a spiritual atmosphere for the day. Or, you may create a sense of closure to your day by offering a bedtime benediction. One helpful approach closes each day with two questions: What was the best thing that happened to me today? What was the worst? How satisfying to end a day by giving God the achievements, by renewing tomorrow's commitments, and by relinquishing frustrating failures or unfinished tasks. Then your mind and spirit will be renewed as you sleep, even as the body is refreshed.

4. Use Bible and Hymnbook Prayers. Try personalizing the Lord's Prayer. Think deeply about the meaning of that brief masterpiece of devotion. Ponder the Fatherhood of

God as you allow the reassuring idea to influence your life. Tell God, "I know You love me more than an earthly parent does." Then ask how you can be a better son or daughter. Think about heaven as you come to the phrase, "Who art in heaven" (RSV). How does the Bible describe heaven?

Try to meet God meaningfully at each part of the Lord's Prayer: adore Him for who He is, cherish each new phrase, and apply its message to your current situation. Let strength flow to your inner world as you remember that Christians from every century have prayed this prayer before you, and rejoice that there is a sense in which your voice mingles with believers from every century, country, and culture. Who says prayer is a lonely task?

As another example, personalize the high-priestly prayer of Jesus in the 17th chapter of John. Notice how Jesus used the word "gave" in verses 6-19. Savor each phrase of this significant prayer as you try to understand what Jesus meant by these words as He came to the end of His earthly ministry. What did the prayer mean to His disciples? What does the prayer mean to you?

Paul's prayer for the Ephesians (3:14-21) may also be used. Note the life-changing concepts in this prayer: "I pray that out of his glorious riches he may strengthen you with power through his Spirit in your inner being, so that Christ may dwell in your hearts through faith."

Another approach is to pray St. Francis' prayer, which has been set to music:

Lord, make me an instrument of Thy peace.
Where there is hatred, let me sow love;
Where there is injury, pardon;
Where there is doubt, faith;
Where there is despair, hope;
Where there is darkness, light;
And where there is sadness, joy.

New vistas of spiritual insights open as you spend a half hour applying Francis' petition to your life.

"Guide Me, O Thou Great Jehovah" is another example of a hymn prayer. The opening line petitions, "Guide me, O Thou great Jehovah, / Pilgrim through this barren land." As you pray the hymn, ask God to help you accept divine leadership. How have you received guidance? How well do you follow His leadership? Next, think of the implications of the praise phrase, "O Thou great Jehovah." Then add, "Pilgrim through this barren land." Turn next to the reassuring line, so full of worship potential, "I am weak, but Thou art mighty; / Hold me with Thy powerful hand" (William Williams).

The spiritual nurture possibilities from the prayers of the Bible and hymnal are nearly limitless. Explore them often to grow spiritually strong.

5. Cultivate Thanks for Trifles and Troubles. Prayer helps us sort the difference between inconveniences and real problems. Since thousands of small blessings add up to make life wonderful, express gratitude for routine provisions like a tasty meal, a friendly letter, a cheery greeting, a baby's grin, or an autumn picnic. Why not make ordinary circumstances or even petty annoyances reasons for thanks?

Try viewing troubles with gratitude. Consider problems as growth opportunities, and pray with thanksgiving for difficulties. A sprained ankle slows you down for reflection, a misunderstanding allows you the grace of giving and receiving forgiveness, and a financial problem teaches deeper dependence on God. A failed business deal, a wait in a doctor's office, or a traffic snarl can be turned into a channel of grace to draw you closer to Christ, to slow you down, or to increase your patience.

Trials often provide teachable moments and valuable lessons. Richard Foster advises, "The dark night is one of the ways God brings us to a hush, a stillness, so that He may work an inner transformation upon the soul."[23]

6. Listen Louder to God. In our impatience and inexperience with silence, we sometimes make prayer monologue rather than dialogue; we fill the time of prayer with a string of high-sounding words rather than letting Scripture resonate within us. The ability to listen, in both the inner and outer life, requires a willingness to hear and a discipline to listen. As Pamela Gray reminds us, "For one soul that exclaims, 'Speak, Lord, for Thy servant heareth,' there are 10 that say, 'Hear, Lord, for Thy servant speaketh.'"[24]

Your life, like most moderns, is probably too noisy. It is difficult to find time or space for reflection when our days start with a ringing alarm and continue with jarring morning news, traffic confusion on the way to work, loud ruckus on the job, and then end with more snarled traffic. Even though the Psalmist never lived with the intensity of our stress, he recommends, "Be still, and know that I am God" (46:10). That means thinking, looking beneath the surface, checking our experiences, and judging our ideas against Scripture. Every disciple of Christ needs to hear God say more about his life.

To be spiritually healthy, a person must occasionally withdraw from the daily grind to a block of quiet time where he drops every hint of resistance and listens with every fiber of his being. Consider Dom Helder Camara's sobering sentence, "The noise that completely smothers the voice of God is the inner uproar of outraged self-esteem, of awakening suspicion, of unsleeping ambition."[25] Those who quiet themselves find recuperative renewal awaiting them in the simple fact that some of life's most confusing riddles can only be solved by intense listening. This exercise makes vital the scriptural directive, "Wait on the Lord" (Ps. 27:14, KJV). To really know God, the bedrock foundation of everything else, takes stillness and time. As Martin Luther explained, "The fewer the words, the better the prayer."[26]

7. Pray All the Time. Dolly of the "Family Circus" cartoon speaks with childlike wisdom when she tells her little brother, "We can talk to God anytime we want because He has a toll-free number."[27] She is right, and we have a special closeness in prayer that takes God into awkward situations when others may be angry, worried, or even unreasonable; it sounds like Steve Harper's idea when he said that John Wesley tuned his "inner voice" to the Creator.[28] Nearly every situation, however tense, can be turned into an inner conversation with the Father—even when others falsely accuse us, when people gossip about us, in the middle of family tensions, and in workplace stresses. Constant contact with Christ lowers stress; the possibilities are magnificent.

8. Recognize a Need for Prayer Breaks. Every feeling of stress or awareness of tension is a signal to pray. Listen carefully for subtle clues that remind you that you need to pray. Because busyness can shrivel the soul, it is important to recognize the desirability of frequent prayer breaks. Our petty reactions to people provide reminders. Nonverbal messages from others may alert us, and sometimes our body informs us that it is time to pray. Another embarrassing hint comes whenever we are forced to make excuses for our conduct. As we keep alert, internal messages remind us when a prayer break is needed.

9. Expand Your Prayer Repertoire. One learns to pray by praying. Experiment with many ways of praying; one may fit your needs better at one time than another. Try adoration, confession, petition, gratitude, and intercession—at least one of these prayer patterns may be unfamiliar to you. Commit yourself to a different kind of prayer each day for a week. You will find spiritual development deepens as your prayer patterns expand; move from mechanics to meditation, from regimentation to relationship, from methods to mastery. Which kind of prayer do you most need? Which prayer pattern is least familiar to you?

God encourages individuality and authenticity when He offers us such a wide range of approaches in our communication with Him. Though monotony, rigidity, and empty forms are deadly enemies of spiritual growth, the disciplines of prayer, worship, and fasting can be vibrant and even liberating. Use variety in prayer to help satisfy your quest to be Christlike.

10. Pray Correction into Your Life. In our most insightful moments, it is refreshingly amazing to realize that I am an unfinished product being drawn to completion by God—someone called it stretching for the stars while standing on the earth. Consequently, during prayer God often identifies improvements He wants us to make as He calls us to something more than a sentimental faith and a lukewarm devotion. Every change the Father proposes must be seen for what it really is—for our good. But Bob Benson is right: "When we pray, we have to change. We have to be different that day. We have to treat people differently. We have to act differently. We walk differently." He continues, for some "it's just easier not to pray. It's just easier not to have His eyes and His heart."[29]

God's insistent nudges toward improvement usually come during quiet prayer, while reading Scripture, in the midst of an unusual life experience, during a chance conversation, while listening to a sermon, or while thinking about the text of a hymn. The Westminster Shorter Catechism summarizes the issue: "Prayer is an offering of our desires unto God, for things agreeable to His will." Caught up in the restless stress of contemporary living, during prayer we discover God's enablement for every correction He urges, so our requests can be shaped into things agreeable to His will.

> *"Our house crashes in ruins because it is not founded on the word of Jesus Christ."*
> —Dietrich Bonhoeffer

10
FOLLOW THE MANUFACTURER'S MANUAL

An eager teenager sounded like an ideal buyer when he phoned about a Toyota I had advertised in the newspaper. He was searching for his first car, to be a 16th-birthday gift from his mother. In spite of mileage and age, our sporty Celica was well maintained because we followed the manufacturer's manual.

Within an hour after his phone call, my young friend brought his mother, an ambitious advertising executive, and his best buddy to check out the car. He expressed delight with the Celica's condition and equipment, which included a five-speed transmission, sporty wheels, a flashy paint job, a top-of-the-line stereo, and an equalizer. He announced with utter amazement on the test drive, "Mom, everything works." In no time, he decided to buy the car. After we settled on a price, his mother wrote a deposit check, and we agreed to transfer title and take delivery the next day. All of this produced tantalizing excitement for this high school buyer and assured me my car would have a good home.

On the spur of the moment, I loaned him the manufacturer's manual until the next day, when it would be his. And I am glad I did.

When they returned, I was astonished at how much this inquisitive teenager taught himself overnight about my Celica. As he slid under the wheel, he knew the location and operation of every system. Motivated by anticipation, he mastered many details from the manufacturer's manual. He discovered that the car's manual provided information about how to make automobile ownership trouble-free and even enjoyable. He learned how fast a Toyota should be driven in each gear, and his questions about tire pressure, fuses, and tune-ups were answered. The manufacturer's manual suggested fine points on how to care for the Toyota even after the owner became familiar with the car.

The Bible, the spiritual development Manufacturer's Manual, does the same for us when it offers instructions on how to live a quality life. Scripture, though not intended as an authority on science or history, provides truth about God and offers insights for making sense out of the puzzling aspect of the human pilgrimage. The Manufacturer's Manual contains amazingly useful guidance for happy adjustment to life and inner wellness.

A skilled technician who loved the Bible because it resourced his living so well was hired to repair a giant telescope. The chief astronomer happened upon the repairman reading his Bible during a lunch break. The scientist scoffed, "What good do you expect to get from the Bible? It is hopelessly out-of-date, and you don't even know who wrote it."

The puzzled repairman inquired after a thoughtful pause, "Do you use the multiplication table around this place? Do you know who wrote it?"

Quickly, the scientist replied, "We use the multiplication table because we know it works."

The repairman replied, "That's why I trust the Bible. It works."

The Manufacturer's Manual—
a Startlingly Unique Book

The Bible works for those who seriously try to understand its message, and it helps readers discover their reason for being. Nothing in the world is as significant to the seeker after God as the day Scripture seizes him, so that the Bible belongs to him and he belongs to the Bible. This happens when readers allow the Bible to speak to their sacred inner center. Like no other literature, its resources are as essential for satisfying living as oxygen, the alphabet, yeast, the sun, or the North Star.

Inasmuch as the Bible deals with both daily experiences and ultimate life-and-death issues, it authoritatively and dynamically challenges every reader including beginners and veterans, students and scholars, young and old, simple and sophisticated, common folks and kings. Designed and preserved by the Father, this faithful old Book nourishes our souls, inspires our minds, and energizes our wills. It tells us more than we could otherwise know about God, life, and ourselves.

The fact that the message of the Bible is so relevant to life surprises many first-time readers and keeps astonishing more frequent readers. It is amazingly up-to-date. Holy Scripture, as a road map out of the complexities of stress, explains how God intended life to function. It deals with the cost and consequences of being, doing, and having—all three have their rewards and disappointments too.

Apparently many moderns think about God only with a mild intellectual curiosity. Perhaps they have not needed the Bible because they have never experienced anguish of soul resulting from sorrow, ambiguity, or sin. Or maybe they never felt perplexed by destructive disappointment or bruised by painful loss. But they will. And when devastating circumstances plunge them into a serious interest in God, the Bible stands ready with strength for the soul.

The Manufacturer's Manual—
a Book of Incredible Influence

Even in contemporary culture, the Bible still has far-reaching influence and surprising impact. Though secularization has clearly infiltrated Western civilization, Scripture still affects modern society. Our language and literature are packed so full of biblical words, phrases, and ideals that no one can talk or think about the basics of life for long without dealing with scriptural ideas. Even secular fields of inquiry like psychology, history, and sociology keep rediscovering that the teachings of Scripture are as true to human experience as studies in their own disciplines.

The Bible influences individuals too. This means that an obedient hearing of Scripture settles many confusions because the Bible calibrates faith with human experience. This potential is underscored by Paul Scherer: "The comfort of the Scriptures never was intended to soothe you or make you feel right, never mind how nasty you've been, or how terrible things are. Rather, it was intended to send you back into the fight, whatever yours happens to be, with all the reinforcements God Almighty himself can throw in."[1] That is exactly what the Bible does when it opens windows of reality and helps us deal with both the bumps and the near-fatal wrecks of the fast track. Scripture calls us to trade tense problems caused by self-sovereignty for God-centered living.

The Manufacturer's Manual—
a Book of Lovers' Quarrels

Students and scholars of Scripture give serious attention to theories about the meaning and origin of the Bible due to the fact that Scripture has such weighty influence on Western civilization, the accompanying development of Christianity, and personal faith. Questions of authorship and dating of original writings have been debated throughout church history and are being discussed even now among church councils, conventions, and general assemblies. The controversies have been so lively for so long that hundreds of books have been published and entire denominations built on a specific theory of Scripture.

Though it is not realistic to expect that any single view about the Bible will be acceptable to everyone, these debates might be viewed as a kind of lovers' quarrel intended to clarify the purpose and meaning of Scripture. Of course, some take the Bible's authority more seriously than others, but anyone who studies Scripture for whatever reason and with whatever motive finds that the Bible judges its readers rather than its being judged by them.

Maybe these debates finally boil down to expressions of abiding affection, perhaps even respect, for the influence the Bible has had on the development of civilization, culture, and personal character. The important reality is that when Scripture is seriously applied to life, it transforms individuals and calls civilizations to righteousness. The Bible continues, as it always has, to nourish the soul and reduce anxious tensions.

After all the profound arguments are finished and the impressive research is published, simple believers, sophisticated scholars, and everyone in between find a wonderful quality of life when they heed the message of Scripture and follow this amazing book to Christ, its Central Character. Reading the Bible helps us know Jesus better. In profoundly significant ways, the Bible changes those who read it, who listen to it, who meditate on it day and night, and who apply it to the details of life.

Legend says when Charles Spurgeon was criticized for not defending the Bible, he humorously replied, "Defend the Bible! I would as soon think of defending a lion. Unchain the Bible, and it will defend itself." At another time and in a different setting, U.S. President Woodrow Wilson explained the far-reaching influence of Scripture: "Give the Bible to the people, unadulterated, pure, unaltered, unexplained, uncheapened, and then see it work through the whole nature."[2] And thousands of years before Spurgeon or Wilson, Jeremiah affectionately announced, "Thy words were found, and I did eat them; and thy word was unto me the joy and rejoicing of mine heart" (Jer. 15:16, KJV). Spurgeon, Wilson, and Jeremiah all agreed that the Bible merely needs application rather than defense. Scripture transforms individuals, families, and even civilization.

The Manufacturer's Manual—an Enduring Book

Written over a 1,500-year time span by approximately 40 authors, the Bible stands as the most enduring book in the history of literature. In spite of this long period of writing, the Bible as a library of 66 books possesses an unprecedented unity not found in other literary collections. To people of every generation for 2,000 years, this miraculous book has communicated God's provisions to make persons holy, useful, and happy. Its uniquely eye-opening characteristics include unity of thought and enormous personal impact.

Any record of the Bible's enchanting longevity shows it has survived fire, apathy, skeptics, disuse, and the recopying efforts of hundreds of scribes. Divine preservation can be observed in its mind-stretchingly accurate transmission, which can be seen by comparing present copies of Scripture with hand-copied manuscripts written before the printing press was invented. This remarkably reliable record infuses stressed people with the assurance that God continues to speak through Scripture to the human dilemma.

Centuries have tested the validity of the Bible's message, and history records how it has redemptively affected millions. The biographies of the saints demonstrate how Scripture decreases anxiety when applied with submissive expectancy to the pressing issues of life. Coming to the Bible always provides personal spiritual benefit when the readers pray with the Psalmist, "Open thou mine eyes, that I may behold wondrous things out of thy law" (119:18, KJV). Now, as always, Scripture illuminates darkness in the soul and lightens burdens in the mind; its endurance is remarkable and its influence incredible.

The Manufacturer's Manual—a Soul Food Book

In many congregations on an average Sunday morning, Scripture offers a staggering range of help for human need, including judgment for ethical issues, comfort for pain, clarity for confusion, inspiration for despair, and discipline for rebellion. William Johnston is right: "The force and power of the word of God is so great that it remains the support and energy of the church, the strength of faith for her children, the food for the soul, and the pure and perennial source of spiritual life."[3] And there is more. All across the world in more private settings, as thousands of individual readers and study groups apply its teaching to their situations, the Bible heals desperate emotional turmoil and spiritual wounds inflicted by stress.

Once I had the good fortune to serve a congregation as pastor where our style and perspectives meshed wonderfully well. One Sunday I preached that the Bible was God's Love Letter to serious spiritual pilgrims who read, digested, and practiced its teachings. Though the sermon could have used more polish, a sense of God's nearness pervaded the sanctuary and elevated all who were part of the worshiping community. During the following week, I received an affirming note from Frances Tullin, one who possesses the lovely gift of encouragement. Part of her letter captured the exact effect Scripture was intended to have on us: "Henceforth, when I open my Bible, I'm sure it will be with a sense of holy hush. May my response always include loving obedience and joyful slavery to Scripture." Frances discovered and summarized several desirable outcomes from Scripture: holy hush quiets the heart in worship, loving obedience makes one eager to follow divine guidance, and joyful slavery sounds like a synonym for wholehearted devotion. That is what diligent readers encounter in Scripture to enable them to be genuinely Christian in all things.

Though evidence abounds that the Bible is no longer read as frequently as it once was, it continues as a readily accessible resource to help reduce stress for contemporary people. The Good Book continues as a best-seller; $170 million was spent for Bibles in the United States in a recent year, and the Gideons place 1 million copies each year in hotels, motels, and hospitals. A few years ago, six new translations were published in one 12-month period, and *Books in Print* listed 55 pages of Bible-related entries, as compared with 15 pages about food and 14 pages related to sex.[4] Copies of Scripture are available everywhere. Nearly everyone in the Western world owns a copy of the Bible or knows where to find one.

Consequently, digesting and practicing the Bible depends on use, not accessibility. As impressive as massive availability sounds, a copy of Scripture on every bookshelf near every hearth is not enough. The Bible must be read if one is to hear the voice of God, get to know Jesus better, and learn how to live. Therefore, the Bible must be taken in hand and read. It must be loved and lived.

The Manufacturer's Manual—a Book to Stifle Stress

Paul wrote these convincing words in a letter to his friends at Rome: "For everything that was written in the past was written to teach us, so that through endurance and the encouragement of the Scriptures we might have hope" (15:4). In one short sentence, the apostle underscores the power of Scripture to instruct us, to resource steadfastness, and to inspire hope. Everyone I know needs all three —instruction, enablement, and inspiration.

Even when the Bible is put to tough tests, it makes good on Paul's promises with soul-stirring guidance that takes the stress out of our bewildering complexities and breaks the grip of our anxieties. Scripture lavishes us with strength so that we can deal with the whirling vortex of tension-related problems. Note the ancient though ever contemporary promises.

As a *relief for loneliness*, Scripture pledges:

"Be strong and of a good courage, fear not, nor be afraid of them: for the Lord thy God, he it is that doth go with thee; he will not fail thee, nor forsake thee" (Deut. 31:6, KJV).

For *frightening fears*, the Bible promises:

"Peace I leave with you, my peace I give unto you: not as the world giveth, give I unto you. Let not your heart be troubled, neither let it be afraid" (John 14:27, KJV).

As an *antidote for anger*, the Word of God instructs:

"For if ye forgive men their trespasses, your heavenly Father will also forgive you" (Matt. 6:14, KJV).

As a *help for frustration*, the Bible guarantees:

"Trust in the Lord with all thine heart; and lean not unto thine own understanding. In all thy ways acknowledge him, and he shall direct thy paths" (Prov. 3:5-6, KJV).

"But they that wait upon the Lord shall renew their strength; they shall mount up with wings as eagles; they shall run, and not be weary; and they shall walk, and not faint" (Isa. 40:31, KJV).

As a *strength in suffering*, Scripture promises:

"For I reckon that the sufferings of this present time are not worthy to be compared with the glory which shall be revealed in us" (Rom. 8:18, KJV).

"Weeping may endure for a night, but joy cometh in the morning" (Ps. 30:5, KJV).

As a *defense for discouragement*, the Word of God provides:

"Be careful for nothing; but in every thing by prayer and supplication with thanksgiving let your requests be made known unto God. And the peace of God, which passeth all understanding, shall keep your minds and hearts through Christ Jesus" (Phil. 4:6-7, KJV).

As an *encouragement during illness,* the Bible assures us:
"Who forgiveth all thine iniquities; who healeth all thy diseases; who redeemeth thy life from destruction; who crowneth thee with lovingkindness and tender mercies; who satisfieth thy mouth with good things; so that thy youth is renewed like the eagle's" (Ps. 103:3-5, KJV).

And in *periods of bereavement,* the Scriptures say:
"Yea, though I walk through the valley of the shadow of death, I will fear no evil: for thou art with me; thy rod and thy staff they comfort me" (Ps. 23:4, KJV).

"Jesus said unto her, I am the resurrection, and the life: he that believeth in me, though he were dead, yet shall he live" (John 11:25, KJV).

These timeless Bible promises offer lifesaving assurances to people who live in a world of secularism where everything seems to be coming loose from its foundation. John Jay Chapman explains this stress-reducing capability of Scripture: "The Bible is a cloud by day and a pillar of fire by night, and the darker the skies grow, whether above an epoch or an individual, the more light it emits."[5] Scripture alleviates anxiety because it deals with essential and changeless values. As a Word-soaked veteran of the way attested, "It is truly true."

What other source offers so many answers for selfishness, lust, greed, and violence? This grand old Book stands true in the contemporary world with solutions to our most difficult problems like reconciliation, love, self-sacrifice, and forgiveness. The Bible has one encompassing message: human beings have problems, but God provides miraculous cures.

The Manufacturer's Manual—
a Book About Quality Living

Scripture awakens and satisfies longings in the soul for God. The Bible, as the main communication channel between God and man, takes us to Christ, who offers comfort for bereavement, rebuke for sin, reenergization for forgotten goals, warning for rebellion, and relief from stress. As an objective written record, it saves God seekers from a tidal wave of private notions about spirituality.

The Bible is a surprisingly simple book, even though some fret over hard-to-understand passages. Some readers are unnecessarily intimidated when their preacher mentions Greek and Hebrew, the original languages of the Scripture. Others wonder about how difficult the Bible may be for them when they start reading complicated passages like the genealogies in Matthew or complexities of Revelation. But anyone, regardless of experience or education, can understand enough of the Bible to discover a new quality of life in relationship with Jesus Christ. The Bible, therefore, continues as a confusing book only to those who do not open its pages.

Conversely, because the riches of Scripture are so inexhaustible, lifelong Bible readers, students, and scholars discover something new each time they read. In both simple and profound ways, the Bible helps readers get better acquainted with Christ as the living Lord speaks through Scripture. Long ago Jesus explained His relatedness to Scripture to the Pharisees, "You search the scriptures, because you think that in them you have eternal life; and *it is they that bear witness to me;* yet you refuse to come to me that you may have life" (John 5:39-40, RSV, italics added).

The written Word, the Bible, takes us to Jesus, the living Word; then God's message flows through paper and ink to help us become intimately acquainted with Christ. The eye-opening implications of this idea show in Frank Laubach's astounding statement that "nine-tenths of the human race would follow Christ if they knew who He is, when they will not follow an abstract truth."[6] That is what the Bible does; it introduces us to Jesus, so that He becomes a living Person for us rather than a theoretical, abstract ideal.

The life and teachings of Jesus connect the Old and

New Testaments. Taken alone, the Old Testament is an incomplete book that looks forward to Christ. Likewise, the New Testament record of the life of Jesus cannot be understood without its Old Testament roots. This interface between Jesus and the Bible shows in Buechner's extraordinary sentence, "I wanted to learn about Christ—about the Old Testament, which had been His Bible, and the New Testament, which was the Bible about Him."[7] This interdependence becomes abundantly clear in the first chapter of Matthew and continues through many direct Old Testament quotations in the New Testament; Bible authorities teach that more than 1,300 Old Testament references and allusions can be found in the New Testament. Thus the Old Testament forms the foundation for the New Testament, even as the New Testament completes the Old Testament.

The Bible guides seekers into holy, happy, useful living—God's strategy for inner wholeness. Paul wrote to Timothy, his son in the ministry, "From infancy you have known the holy Scriptures, *which are able to make you wise for salvation through faith in Christ Jesus*" (2 Tim. 3:15, italics added). The Psalmist led Old Testament congregations in singing, "How can a young man keep his way pure? *By living according to your word*" (119:9, italics added). The ancient hymn writer continued, "I have hidden your word in my heart *that I might not sin against you*" (v. 11, italics added). The Bible claims to be a source for holistic living: "All scripture is given by inspiration of God, and is *profitable for doctrine, for reproof, for correction, for instruction in righteousness:* that the man of God may be perfect, throughly furnished unto all good works" (2 Tim. 3:16-17, KJV, italics added). According to this record, God's prescribed path to wholeness is inner purity.

The Bible, as a sourcebook for healing stress, makes us see ourselves as we actually are. Heb. 4:12 says, "The word of God is quick, and powerful, and sharper than any twoedged sword, piercing even to the dividing asunder of soul and spirit, and of the joints and marrow, and is a *discerner of the thoughts and intents of the heart*" (KJV, italics added). But the seeker after God need not be frightened by this new self-awareness because the Bible also shows him how to close the gap between who he is and who he can become. The Bible helps eliminate the tension between being and becoming by making both possible and enjoyable. From Scripture, the serious seeker finds the path to a quality life; then serenity replaces stress.

The Manufacturer's Manual—a Demanding Book

Though not advertised on Main Street, many find the Bible stifling and boring. This happens because they read an occasional fragment for tradition's sake, though they prefer novels, newspapers, magazines, or television. At the other end of the spectrum, some insist they must have frequent contact with the Bible; for them, it is a fascinatingly helpful book that speaks to their emotional, intellectual, and spiritual concerns. Obedient yieldedness makes the difference even when the Bible's truth is uncomfortable.

Though other books can be read at whatever level of intensity the reader chooses for instruction, information, techniques, or pleasure, this Book pressures individuals to master its message. Precisely at this point, the Bible is significantly different from all other books because it only renews and enriches those who read with a yielded yes. Nothing is more vital to the ability to understand Scripture than wholehearted devotion to Christ. When out of tune with God, the inner world is cluttered with self-centered sin, harbored resentments, and neglected spiritual opportunities. In contrast, a clean inner life sharpens one's ability to hear the message of Scripture so that he can escape the enslavement of "what is" to move on to the point of "what can be." Useful techniques allow the Bible to nourish the inner world.

- **Start simply.** Beginners should think of the Bible as a library of books, so no one need commence at Genesis and read through Revelation. At the onset of a spiritual quest, it is useful to browse through this 66-book library until a section captures one's interest and speaks to one's need. A plan for those who are new to Scripture might begin with Matthew 5—7 (the Sermon on the Mount); Psalms 23, 24, 100, 122, 139; Isaiah 35, 55; the Gospels of Mark and Luke; or Paul's letter to the Philippians. Next, begin cultivating a friendship with Old Testament prophets like Jeremiah, Amos, Hosea, or Micah. Then, turn to the Acts of the Apostles in the New Testament for exciting accounts of the Early Church. After completing these sections, the reader will be ready for almost any passage.

• **Take time.** History records stalwart saints who arose as early as four o'clock in the morning to read Scripture. Others read all night. Though their examples do not offer precise patterns for today, they do demonstrate that spiritual development requires us to take quality time for Bible reading. It is time well spent because every relationship and responsibility go better after such a saturation with God's way of thinking.

It is more desirable to invest 15 prime minutes per day than to wait to have longer, sporadic spurts. Why not move past yesterday's failures about Bible reading and begin a vital relationship now? Free yourself from the patterns others suggest to develop a workable method of your own.

• **Read with anticipation.** To counteract boredom, count on receiving a fresh word from God each time you read. Anticipation nourishes one's readiness to listen and learn. Persons who look for a fresh word from Scripture are seldom disappointed. Receptivity always expands as new truth is allowed into the shady nooks and obscure corners of life. Those who expect the Bible to speak to their situation usually discover a gold mine of stress-reducing resources.

• **Read in spite of feelings.** Everyone has mood swings that fluctuate for no apparent reason. To keep from being victimized by moods, every individual should read the Bible when he feels like it, when he does not feel like it, and when he has no feelings. How encouraging during down moods to read the psalm, "My soul melteth for heaviness: strengthen thou me according unto thy word" (119:28, KJV).

- **Read for meanings.** The Bible, though not a good-luck charm, is a tender letter from the Enlightener who knows everything. Thus, the God seeker should read the Bible until it says something significant to him. While it may seem desirable to read 10 verses, two chapters, or a whole book at one sitting, it is generally more rewarding to read until the Bible speaks to your situation. Stop and listen to key words, phrases, verses, or paragraphs; a meeting of meanings is more important than prescribed procedure.

Keep reading in spite of difficult passages. Follow Spurgeon's advice when you come to a puzzling passage: "When I am eating fish and come upon a bone, I don't fling the whole fish away. I put the bone on the side of the plate so that I can go on enjoying the fish." Take time to seek clarification from commentaries, atlases, dictionaries, and other study aids. Keep reading. Think of Scripture as God's personal word to you for each day.

- **Share it.** One gifted Bible teacher said, "I learned what I know about the Bible by teaching it." Home Bible studies, family devotions, Bible classes, and even casual conversation offer opportunities to encourage others with Scripture. A shared word from the Bible frequently relieves personal perplexity. To offer a promise from Scripture provides a lift for the giver and keeps the receiver thinking about the passage for a long time, so both are energized by its message.

To encourage lifelong growth, remember two characteristics of Scripture that stand forever: the Bible is simple enough that anyone can find his way to God and challenging enough to stimulate the most brilliant mind.

How to Use the Bible to Lower Stress

The Bible, a living, 2,000-year-old book, is the most useful resource for quality living available to the human family. It will continue to serve as a promise of God's faithfulness as long as people remain on earth. Scripture keeps amazing folks, like the brilliant college freshman who knows everything until he meets a wise old person who tells him how life really works. The Bible does that. It is full of wisdom and truth to help readers deal with life as it is. But how can we maximize these benefits?

1. Personalize a Passage. Read until you receive a word that speaks to your situation. Put your name in the promise as you read: "I will never leave [your name] nor forsake [your name]" (Heb. 13:5, KJV). "Who shall separate [your name] from the love of Christ? shall tribulation, or distress, or persecution, or famine, or nakedness, or peril, or sword?" (Rom. 8:35, KJV). "I will not leave [your name] as orphans; I will come to [your name]" (John 14:18).

Personalize a passage by allowing it to take you to Jesus. This can be done by reading what our Lord did or said in the Gospels. Then contrast what you do and say in similar circumstances. Few experiences are so humbling, but it provides healing medicine for complacency or selfishness.

Another way to make Scripture your own is to pray it back to God. On your knees, with your Bible open to a passage, simply pray, "Lord, I think this passage promises help for my present problem." Or "Lord, this passage makes demands I cannot meet. I need Your help now." Or "Lord, open the meaning of this passage for me. Overcome my slow mind and active resistance. I want the mind of Christ." This method harmonizes belief with behavior as a reader moves from merely reading the Bible to actually living it.

2. Enter Scripture as an Active Participant. Look at a miracle, an event, a parable, a relationship, or even a single word through the eyes of the people who were there. Allow its first meaning to take root in you. Seek to apply all your senses to help you live the experience and listen for its contemporary significance. How did Lazarus feel as he threw off his graveclothes? What would it be like to rub shoulders and dispositions with Peter and John? As you read Jeremiah, think how troubled his times seemed to him. How would it feel to be in prison with Paul? Or, what was the leper's reaction when Jesus healed him?

As an example, in your mind climb into the tree with Zacchaeus to get a better view of Jesus. Try to imagine every detail of that event. See, hear, and smell the pressing crowd. Feel the burning heat. Grip the tree limb. Sneeze in the swirling dust. Then allow your heart to melt with devotion as Jesus calls your name and invites himself to your home. Be an active participant who views the incident as if it happened yesterday or today.

3. Develop a Personal Bible Study Method. Try to discover a method that works well for you. The SMA method, both simple and useful, unlocks a passage with three questions: What does it *say*? What does it *mean*? How can it be *applied* to life? (S = say; M = mean; A = apply.)

A second technique uses three time dimensions: *Then* (exegesis) asks what the original writer meant when the passage was first written; *always* (exposition) asks what truth in this passage applies to human situations in every age; and *now* (application) asks what the passage says to your own situation. That trio—then, always, and now—can be counted on to open the meaning of the Bible.

Another helpful approach is to follow Terry Hall's suggestion that a person write a short summary title for each chapter of Scripture in his own study Bible. His guidelines for labeling each chapter are: (1) Use four words or less, (2) discover the original thought of the writer, (3) consider the chapter's uniqueness, and (4) retain the big idea.[8] This approach allows readers to relate each chapter to their lives, consider how the paragraphs fit together, and summarize the chapter's meaning. It also provides a study guide for subsequent readings.

Effective Bible study begins with an assumption that the paragraph is the basic study unit that deals with one central idea. These sections, marked with a paragraph symbol in the King James Version, have regular paragraph indentations in newer translations. Though there are many powerful single verses, it always deepens one's understanding of Scripture to study each passage in the context of a paragraph, chapter, or entire book.

4. Participate Seriously in Biblical Preaching. Accurate hearing of a sermon is as important as preaching one. The communication process is like the sound of a falling tree in a remote forest; while it can be argued that a falling tree made a crashing sound, nothing was communicated if no one heard. In the same way, preaching must be heard to be effective. Wholehearted participation by the listener requires serious mental, emotional, and spiritual engagement with the biblical passage, the preacher's thoughts, and the implications of the sermon.

Why not consider sermons as a source to help you better understand Scripture? Persons who attend worship services every Sunday morning receive 26 hours of Bible teaching each year (52 sermons x 30 minutes of preaching), and those who attend an additional service each week double the impact. Think of the possibilities for stress reduction when one experiences 52 hours of biblical instruction each year for a lifetime. In this way, the promise that faith comes by hearing (Rom. 10:17) becomes an actuality, and special blessing is promised to those who read, hear, and heed (Rev. 1:3).

This kind of sermon hearing, much more than courteous listening, requires tough mental engagement with the biblical content of the sermon while it is being preached and long after it is finished. Since the sermon preached and the sermon heard are never identical, the listener may go back to the Scripture to check meanings. A clarification might even be requested from the preacher; he will be gratified to know someone gave his sermon a second thought. Such a shared reception of Scripture bonds listener and preacher together in a passion for the truth as found in the Bible.

5. Cultivate a Berean Attitude. When Paul preached at Berea, "They received the message with great eagerness and *examined the Scriptures every day to see if what Paul said was true*" (Acts 17:11, italics added). Such resolute study makes the Bible come to life, so that each reading offers additional insights for life. Such reading need not be the critical analysis of a prosecuting attorney as much as a receptive reading by a single-minded disciple with a mood of openness that asks, "What does God want me to hear from this passage?"

The Berean plan can be personalized by writing your discoveries in a letter to God. The main divisions of such a letter might include: (1) Thank You, Lord, for what I learned from this passage; (2) help me correct my life according to this scripture; and (3) I confess the shortcomings I learned from this passage. These letters can be kept in a journal to provide a satisfying record of spiritual progress resulting from encounters with the Bible. Over several weeks, as you mesh the details of your life with the teachings of Scripture, your spiritual development will astound you.

6. Try the Six Questions Exercise. This method builds on the journalist's five Ws and one H formula, which Rudyard Kipling summarized in *Just-So Stories:*

I keep six honest serving-men
(They taught me all I knew);
Their names are What and Why and When
And How and Where and Who.

Question biblical passages with who, what, when, where, why, and how. The answers will transform your inner world and deepen the meaning of Scripture for you.

7. Paraphrase a Passage. This exercise helps you learn

more about life from Scripture because it requires you to carefully consider the meaning of every word in the passage. Chaplain Carl F. Burke, who served for years in a boys' correctional institution near Buffalo, N.Y., used this technique to make Scripture relevant to delinquent boys from urban slums. Think how one 11-year-old was affected by his own paraphrase of a portion of Psalm 23: "The Lord is my probation officer. He will help me. He tries to help me make it every day. He makes me play it cool."[9]

Ask yourself as you read, What does the passage say to me? To be most effective, this approach requires that paraphrases be written—writing encourages organization and precision of thought. Some people keep a journal where they record paraphrases and jot down new thoughts for future reading. To write your paraphrase now and read it later deepens its impact and makes you deal with the passage at least twice. In reality, two or more thoughtful encounters with a passage make it reverberate in the inner world for a long time. Likely, this practice will lead to the joyous discovery that obedience to Scripture is more than a duty but is also a gloriously satisfying adventure.

8. Make Friends of Bible Personalities. Every reader remembers an especially influential biographical article or book about a famous person like Washington, Lincoln, Churchill, Truman, or Kennedy that shaped their views of democracy and patriotism. Likewise, Bible personalities like Elijah, Joseph, Paul, and Peter help us know God better and mold our thoughts about forgiveness, hope, and faith.

Biblical characters can be studied around their strengths, sins, crises, or spiritual influences. The enormous enablement these individuals received from God in the midst of illusions and ambiguities may be the exact encouragement you need to see you through your current perplexities. How reassuring to learn that at least one Bible character lived through stress just like yours.

9. Use Your Knowledge of Scripture. Like all skills,

learning about Scripture expands as it is used. That is why memorized Scripture is easier to retain when it is recited frequently; hearing a sermon becomes more meaningful when it is practiced in life; and discussing the Bible increases one's understanding of its message.

Those who communicate the Bible in teaching, preaching, and witnessing need to internalize its message before they share it. Some serious disciples consider their understanding and use of the Bible as an ascending seven-step ladder: (1) hear, (2) read, (3) study, (4) memorize, (5) reflect, (6) apply, and (7) share.[10] Each step strengthens all subsequent efforts.

10. Compare Translations. The purpose of translations is to deliver the Bible's message to ordinary people in words they understand. For many the stately, familiar King James Version, first published in 1611, still remains the best-known, much-loved, and often-used version; for years to come it will doubtless remain their first choice. But new translations open the meaning of Scripture to this generation and communicate its wisdom in words used on Main Street. Modern translations update words that may have changed in nearly four centuries and take advantage of newly discovered older manuscripts, which were written nearer the date of the original writings. These are the reasons why new translations may explain the original writer's message more accurately.

Try using various translations to help you trace themes like love, faith, or hope throughout the entire Bible; a concordance or study Bible will help locate the references. The Bible's comprehensive message on these big themes will prove to be an antidote to anxiety and stress.

Consider reading a whole book of the Bible at one sitting, even as you would read a whole mystery or listen to an entire concerto. Such an encounter with a book of the Bible opens new understandings and provides a deeper acquaintance with the writer.

As you compare individual passages in various translations, make a commitment to be as thorough as possible in your study of Scripture. John Wesley once received a letter informing him, "The Lord has told me to tell you that He doesn't need your book-learning, your Greek, and your Hebrew." Wesley replied, "Thank you, Sir. I already knew the Lord had no need for my 'book-learning,' as you put it. However—although the Lord has not directed me to say so—on my own responsibility I would say to you that the Lord does not need your ignorance, either."[11]

Serious study of Scripture can be splendid and thorough at the same time. There need be no contradiction between tenderheartedness and tough thought; God welcomes both as sojourners seek to faithfully follow the Manufacturer's Manual. Your life will be more useful and joyful as you follow God's instruction in Scripture. The Bible, much more than a mere book, is a way of life, an encounter with God, a loving correspondence of the Father's plans for His child, and a revelation of what really matters. The Bible is an invitation to fulfillment and a promise of enablement for the authentically good life—an effective way out of stress.

Exercises to Strengthen the Heart

*"When you admit Jesus into your heart, nothing is
predictable but everything becomes possible."*
—Henri J. M. Nouwen

11

Exercises to Make Your Heart like His

State law required a physical exam on my way to youth camp because I had been drafted at the last minute to serve as a counselor for 10-year-old boys. The physician joked as he checked my chest X ray, "I can't see your heart." When I reported the doctor's comment to my friend who was traveling to camp with me, he retorted, "That's easy to understand—a black heart like yours is always hard to see on X rays."

Later as we drove along, my friend discussed a heartbreaking problem in a family we knew. Soon after arriving at camp, the director called a staff meeting to deal with the heart of an administrative problem. Another volunteer could not come to camp because his mother had suffered a heart attack. That day, like most days, that word *heart* kept following us around as we tried to make sense of life.

The physical heart, as familiar as the beating of our pulse, yet as mysterious as our awareness of God, consists of an incredible bundle of muscles and nerves located at left of the center in the chest behind the rib cage. About the size of a fist, this cardiac wonder—so small to do so much—pumps millions of gallons of blood through the body for a lifetime. This amazing source of physical life keeps a person alive from quickening in his mother's womb until the final second of earthly existence. For good reason, medical science now believes that stress affects the health of your heart and your risk of developing—or even dying from—cardiac disease.

The word *heart*, however, has a significantly wider meaning connected with spiritual well-being. Heart, in the spiritual sense, is more than a description of the physical, emotional, or intellectual components of living; it embraces all three and involves much more. Heart has to do with the essence of Christlike humanness, the center of our being, and the seedbed for spiritual development.

When rational, emotional, physical, and spiritual dimensions of living are combined, it is easy to see that the word *heart* is always at the center of stress in some way, even as it is always at the core of faith development. Everyone understands how the cardiac muscle determines physical vitality with 4,000 contractions per minute for a lifetime. And researchers believe the health of your heart and vascular system are at least partly determined by what is on your mind; in other words, scientists are only now beginning to discover what poets and saints have always known.

Though the spiritual formation side may not be so obvious, a pure heart at the core of character is what makes meaning, significance, and fulfillment possible. Interestingly, my friend's remark about my black heart on the way to camp underscores the way the cardiac and character dimensions converge and affect each other. Stress is a common denominator in psychiatry, cardiology, and spirituality.

To clarify these issues, more data must be considered. In the Bible, heart refers to the inward place of thinking, loving, and deciding—the place where affection, emotion, passion, conscience, and faith meet and grow together. Heart refers to the center of moral, spiritual, and intellectual life—the seat of emotions, beliefs, and decisions. Since this word *heart* refers to the hidden depth of life, stress must be clearly more than a mere ailment of the physical heart. From beginning to end, the human experience compels us to give extra attention to the scriptural proverb that unites the physical and spiritual dimensions of a satisfying life: "A heart at peace gives life to the body" (Prov. 14:30).

Jesus diagnosed heart ailments when He quoted Isaiah with approval, "These people honor me with their lips, but their hearts are far from me" (Mark 7:6). These words, to His hearers and to us, undercut enslaving attention to external customs, regulations, traditions, rituals, and rules. Those same words also teach the inwardness of spirituality, based on the assumption that a good heart produces authentically Christian attitudes and actions. All this helps us understand that just as the physical heart is the propelling force of blood to keep the human body healthy, the Christ-centered inner heart is the enabling source for wholeness in the moral, spiritual, and intellectual dimensions of life.

In pointing the way to the truly good life of Christ-centeredness, a seasoned old minister preached, "The matter of the heart is the heart of the matter." Amazingly, every difficulty of the heart—physical, emotional, or spiritual—produces some degree of stress. Conversely, spirituality always lowers and sometimes eliminates anxious tension. That is why our thinking about the heart must take in all of life if we want to experience the full possibilities of inner wellness. Therefore, a regimen of exercise and prevention to produce a strong spiritual heart includes the intentional application of love, faith, and hope to details of daily existence. The choice is stress or spirituality, despair or trust, anxiety or confidence.

A Heart Transplant—Begin with Conversion

The conversion issue, God's offer of a revolutionary new beginning, must be faced before spiritual development can be considered seriously. Christianity, according to Paul Scherer's wise observation, has "for 2,000 years been hawking its wares: New lives for old! If it cannot make good there, it cannot make good, period! That is what it is about. And it is about nothing else."[1] True spirituality begins with a life-changing encounter with Jesus Christ, a kind of spiritual heart transplant that integrates the inner world and gives meaning to the outer world.

With stunning accuracy, Jesus diagnosed a universal need in Nicodemus, a distinguished religious leader. Using plain words, Christ called His cure a new birth. To this day a sense of hope excites seekers as they read this candid conversation between Jesus and Nicodemus (John 3:1-21); in this happy incident they see themselves and God. Simply but significantly stated, conversion so radically changes human character that new values shape thought and behavior. This transformation impacts life at its deepest level; far from diminishing life, conversion leads into a deeper relationship with God, and with it comes an indescribable awareness of integration and peace.

Such an encounter with Christ profoundly impacted Leo Tolstoy, the Russian novelist, who explained his faith journey in his book *My Religion:* "Five years ago faith came to me; I believed in the doctrine of Jesus, and my whole life underwent a sudden transformation. What I had once wished for I wished for no longer, and I began to desire what I had never desired before. What had once appeared to me right now became wrong, and the wrong of the past I beheld as right. . . . My life and my desires were completely changed; good and evil interchanged meanings."[2]

Conversion does that for everyone; it revolutionizes commitments and transforms values, so that the family traits of Jesus show up in character and conduct. Oswald Chambers states his bottom line conviction, "If Jesus Christ cannot alter a man's disposition, Christianity is a cunningly devised fable."[3] And he is right.

Human beings, without Christ as Center, are likely to

encounter such confusion and stress that they become unsatisfied secularists, or they start to chase religious fads, new cults, or charming gurus. Though it is fashionable to classify oneself around religious labels like Catholic, Methodist, Baptist, Lutheran, or charismatic, it is easy to embrace a religious system without a Savior or agree to doctrinal propositions without the Person. E. Stanley Jones, the influential Methodist missionary to India, believed many "know about God but do not know Him; are informed about Christ but are not transformed by Him; know about moral laws but are powerless to fulfill them."[4] Apparently thousands live by the untested assumption that everything will work out if they are good all their lives. This seductive theory lulls people into mushy religion that produces absolutely no impact on daily life.

True conversion, in contrast, transforms low-grade stress about nebulous religion into vital faith. It calls everyone to the adventure of integrating the human journey around Christ who requires a person to live life His way. Erasmus, an aide to the Reformers of the early 16th century, explained, "By a Carpenter mankind was made, and only by that Carpenter can mankind be remade."[5] This conversion encounter makes it possible to trade trivial pursuits for a purposeful pilgrimage with the living Christ and opens the clenched fist to accept God's helping hand.

Meaning starts at conversion and dramatically increases as spiritual development follows.

Heart Therapy—Talk to Yourself

People talk to themselves—watch drivers at stoplights or pedestrians as they walk along. Internal conversations, which no one sees or hears, are even more common. These interior discussions have power to shackle or free us as we analyze situations, question experiences, debate alternatives, reinforce fears, and cultivate dreams. Evidently every human being possesses the ability to talk himself into a full-blown case of tension by using deceptive self-dialogue. On the contrary, Christ-centered self-talk remedies stress.

Destructive inner monologues make us believe malicious lies or reinforce old, entrenched attitudes. This happens when injurious information, like a worthless antique phonograph record, gets stored in our minds for instant replay at a moment's notice. We replay the old script and for some self-defeating reason we enjoy the words, sing the sad melodies, and remember the old pain; we even experience the old suffering. Some self-talk recordings keep repeating, "Don't try because you always fail." Others remind us, "You can do no wrong because you have always been special."

This information out of our past tries to convince us that we are too tall, too short, too young, too old, too stupid, too smart, or too something. Then we believe crippling notions like, "You ruined your life by marrying the wrong person," or "You are a bad parent because of your rebellious children." Surprisingly, many of these overused records were started in us by people who have been in the cemetery for decades.

Self-talk proves to be especially seductive for those in positions of authority or leadership. Just because an individual has dominant control as a parent, city official, lay church leader, boss, physician, bishop, club president, or senator does not mean the individual is right or that his decisions are helpful to those he leads. Conscientious leaders, therefore, need to ask themselves, "Am I doing what God wants in this situation? Am I fair? Am I seeking the well-being of those I lead?" Such self-interrogation increases a leader's authenticity and decreases the possibility of self-deception.

For some strange reason, some individuals prefer self-delusion to seeing facts as they are. Could John W. Gardner's startling sentence be true: "More often than not we don't want to know ourselves, don't want to depend on ourselves, don't want to live with ourselves."[6] If his assessment is even partly accurate, honest self-talk is desperately needed to help us cope with modern life. To make self-talk useful, try eavesdropping on yourself to get rid of destructive inner statements like "I'm dumb, stupid, lazy, or weak." Add ideas like "love" and "I can do it." Allow your self-talk, like a conversation with a trusted friend, to question your exaggerations, explore alternative solutions, and commend your strengths. Give yourself a pep talk based on your faith and aspirations. You control the self-doubting voice within.

To speak the truth to yourself, check the facts and challenge your assumptions. Ask yourself, "Am I creating a problem or keeping it going to get sympathy, gain attention, or get even with someone?" Admit vulnerability. Resist self-pity because it generally builds on unreliable data originating from limited perspective or personal prejudices. Using happy memories, replay good times. Add ideas like challenge and opportunity. Remind yourself that accurate self-talk is a tool for converting stress into strength.

To practice constructive self-talk, try conversations like these:

"I am God's creation, and He does not make junk."

"I always do my best. Sometimes that is not good enough. But everyone makes mistakes."

"I have a missing Center of spirituality, but I intend to find Him."

"I can control my reactions; I refuse to let other people ruin my day."

"I have problems with authority over other folks, but I can improve."

"I am needed by someone."

"I am making a valuable contribution to my family."

There is a strong likelihood that accurate self-talk may lead to confession, which brings forgiveness and generates strength for a new start. An old preacher shared an important stress-reducing technique: "You always get further with God when you tattle on yourself."

Heart Treatment—Accept Duplicity in Others and Avoid It in Yourself

Duplicity stresses many people. Life is not always fair; hard work does not always result in appropriate rewards; and fair play sometimes counts for nothing. Ruined reputations or poor results can flow from pure intentions. Trusted friends may turn into Judas traitors. Good people sometimes shade the truth in the name of expediency or gentility. And seasoned disciples sometimes revert to old ways.

The possibility of duplicity, an essential disharmony between one's inner self and outer self, exists in every relationship. William Blake warns: "A truth that is told with bad intent / Beats all the lies you can invent."[7] It happens with frightening frequency. Children deceive parents. Parents mislead children. Some young professionals scheme to get undeserved promotions. Media reporters slant news to fit personal bias. Civic leaders choose cheap politics in place of statesmanship. Some physicians are motivated more by money than by healing the sick. Duplicity even exists in the church.

Confusing double-dealing is not new, however. Even during the earthly ministry of Jesus, religious leaders who professed a high interest in truth tried to trick Him with loaded questions about Jewish customs. Their pretended concern for Sabbath laws had almost nothing to do with their hidden agenda; their questions were calculated traps intended to undercut His revolutionary impact on their vested interests. Eventually, double speech exposed their insecure schemes and downright wickedness.

The apostle Paul experienced similar difficulties. From jail he acknowledged that some preachers proclaimed Christ out of envy and rivalry, supposing they could stir up trouble while he was imprisoned. This duplicity, however, had little effect on the apostle, who concluded, "What does it matter? The important thing is that in every way, whether from false motives or true, Christ is preached. And because of this I rejoice" (Phil. 1:18).

Many painful examples of mixed motives can be found in Scripture, church history, and personal experience. Why, then, should we be surprised to find seeds of duplicity in every human contact?

After admitting the existence of duplicity, stress can be significantly lessened by taking a nonjudgmental attitude toward those who perpetuate it. Jesus insisted that judging another's intentions is God's work alone. Perhaps His reasons take into account our offense at such lack of integrity, the ultimate fairness of God, and our frail inability to understand all the facts.

Three important issues must be remembered about judging: (1) Our assessment may be wrong, (2) the possibility of self-deception, and (3) the fact that we are not ultimately responsible for another. Because conduct-shaping factors sometimes trick even the most conscientious, Thomas Merton claims, "Every one of us is shadowed by an illusory person: a false self."[8] He is right; who is not at least partially confused when asked, "Why did you do what you did?" or "Why did you say what you said?"

Immeasurable help for dealing with duplicity, both in others and ourselves, comes as we pray with C. S. Lewis, "May it be the real I who speaks; may it be the real Thou that I speak to."[9]

How then can the frustration caused by duplicity be reduced? Begin by cherishing the lofty intentions and generous actions of those you have known. Pattern your life after God's gracious forgiveness, and give up your judgments about other people. Try to forget the imperfections of others. As a result, crippling tensions will decrease because your energy will no longer be invested in assigning blame for duplicity. Inner peace, then, is nourished in our inner world when we leave others and their motives to God without judgment. Wholehearted acceptance of all we meet comes when we assume that duplicity in other people originates from confused motives rather than intentional deceit.

For ourselves, however, we must keep asking, Are my words something I would say to Jesus? And would He see through my wrongheadedness, my revenge, my self-defense, and my conformity? His forgiveness makes me willing to overlook double dealing in others. But in myself, I must face the fact that Jesus is always what He says He is, and I must work with the premise that the Lord expects the same in me.

Heart Exercise—Refurbish Your Inner World

"Instead of waiting for someone to bring flowers, plant your own garden and decorate your soul" is good advice from an anonymous writer. Hanging on the wall of Mother Teresa's clinic, The Place of the Pure Heart—Home for Dying Destitutes, is a verse written by a Hindu poet:

If you have two pieces of bread,
Give one to the poor,
Sell the other,
And buy hyacinths
To feed your soul.[10]

Assuming everyone agrees the soul needs to be refurbished, how is it to be done? Some recommend that assertiveness, dominance, and intimidation should reign as ruling king of our attitudes and thoughts. According to this line of reasoning, Christian qualities like self-denial, servanthood, and humility are worthless. Such guidance, however, only frustrates weak people who are told to be strong. They wonder how they can pull themselves up by their bootstraps when they have no boots.

In many ways, spiritual development is like other types of self-help because it requires a great deal of personal effort. But there is one important difference—spirituality supplies sufficiency. That means partnership with Deity provides enablement at the same time as it encourages an awareness of our importance to God. Then, fear of the future fades with the knowledge that the Helper will be in every tomorrow. Freedom to live the way God planned—with His help—is a thousand times more satisfying than doing our own thing.

God offers many underused disciplines for refurbishing the inner life. At first, these resources sound overly simple, so something bigger, newer, and more sophisticated is sought. But Merton explains, "The really new is that which, at every moment, springs freshly into new existence. What is really new is what was there all the time."[11]

Therefore, just as a mature vocabulary uses a simple alphabet, true inner refurbishing starts and continues with the old but ever-new exercises of prayer, Bible reading, and meditation. Anyone can use these resources to refurbish his inner world. They are ours for the using; what God provides is all we need.

Heart Healing—Deal with Addictions

Addictions of a thousand varieties overstress contemporary people, and we feel anxious about the way they affect our friends, our family, and us. Addiction, defined, is any fixation of mind or body that commands so much importance that normal functioning is not possible and spiritual development is neglected or nonexistent. The list of possible addictions is long. Nearly everyone is hooked on one or more compulsions; it could be too much jogging, reading, working, or housecleaning. Addictions result from destructive habits that need to be corrected by a sense of balance in the ways we spend our time, energy, and money.

The damage caused by alcohol, nicotine, and narcotics is obvious; but what about misused prescriptions and food as the drug of choice? Not-so-obvious addictions range from negative attitudes to feelings of inadequacy to being a workaholic. Television addictions range from soap operas to sports to religious programming. Athletic events can enslave participants and spectators. Gossip addiction causes good people to believe unfounded rumors, judge neighbors, and read scandalous newspapers or questionable magazines. Others are bound by addictions that pass for normal behavior, like an unquenchable desire for prestige or money. Though these addictions may not visibly chain people, they cause serious handicaps nevertheless.

Addictions create barriers to wholeness that tense the body, dull the mind, and shackle the soul. The first commandment calls for renunciation of lesser gods, even those that appear to be insignificant to us; the Hebrews Epistle urges us to desert besetting sins (12:1, KJV); and an Indian proverb instructs individuals to "call on God, but row away from the rocks."[12]

Uncontrolled appetites for food, alcohol, sex, money, power, or anything else ultimately destroy individuals. Though an addiction may taste sweet, it is a deadly poison nonetheless. That was Adam and Eve's problem in the garden.

Therefore, if one is to enjoy a genuinely quality life, both subtle and blatant hindrances must be pruned. Paul's firm resolve must be ours, "I will not be mastered by anything" (1 Cor. 6:12). That is the reason why Susanna Wesley taught her children these lessons from Thomas à Kempis: "Whatever weakens your reason, impairs the tenderness of your conscience, obscures your sense of God, or takes off the relish of spiritual things; in short, whatever increases the strength and authority of your body over your mind—that thing is sin to you, however innocent it may be in itself."[13] The advice is valid in every generation for all ages. One stops by stopping, aided by the resources God provides. Corrupting addictions must be deserted if one wants to enjoy a healthy heart and a singing soul.

Heart Exercise—Turn Duty to Delight

Nagging reminders of duty lurk in many corners of our minds. The buzzwords—*oughts* and *shoulds*—create inner strife when used by parents, spouses, children, bosses, pastors, or teachers. Strange but true, we even use ought and should on ourselves. Perhaps the taproot of this stress starts when children are taught that good manners and saved allowances are absolute necessities for a satisfying life. Or the seeds of this tension may begin when harassed teachers try to civilize a class by scolding those who talk and punishing those who do not finish their work on time. Though the origin makes interesting speculation, the reality of this fixation of duty causes second-class living for lots of folks.

Inasmuch as responsibilities cannot be denied, how can these stifling feelings about duty be avoided? Start by cultivating a perspective that turns duty into delight; examples include marriage, parenting, and vocation.

Though the marriage ideal has been severely shattered in much of contemporary society, it starts and continues by keeping serious vows for a lifetime. Marriage is indeed an obligation, but it is also a wonderful privilege that nourishes our inborn hunger for closeness. This enriching obligation turns to delight when both spouses see marriage as an adventure to help them be fulfilled human beings together.

A child, the fruit of his parents' love, imposes demanding long-term responsibilities that begin with a birth cry and last until death separates generations. Potential parenting tensions continue or even increase through preschool nurturing, grade school demands, teenage development, and young adult independence. But so much more is possible. If they look for it, parents can experience continuing joy at every point of the journey. Few things are more satisfying than forging life-lasting bonds with one's children.

Jobs offer another opportunity to develop wholesome perspectives about duty. In modern society, time and skills are pledged for paychecks, so the way a person views work substantially affects his satisfaction with life. Some workers dislike their jobs so much that they constantly fret about how life evaporates for them even as they mark time until next Friday, another vacation, retirement, or they suffer some disability. There must be a better way. Who wants a physician, mechanic, preacher, or pharmacist who views his work as dreary drudgery?

Occupations can be expressions of service to fellow human beings and to God. On this point, one spiritual master suggested, "Work occupies the body and mind and is necessary for health of the spirit. Work can help us pray, if we work properly."[14] The difference between delight and drudgery takes place as we infuse meaning into our work. An unexpected inner force energizes those who do their work with joy, so the promise becomes a reality, "I can do all things through Christ which strengtheneth me" (Phil. 4:13, KJV).

Every individual is obligated to himself to find ways to change duty to fulfillment and responsibility to meaning. Begin by seeking to build satisfying purpose into your responsibilities; as a consequence, your body will benefit from a slower heart rate, deeper breathing, and relaxed muscles. Other advantages may include a happier family, a satisfied boss, content customers, and an easygoing relationship with coworkers.

Heart Exercise—Choose Your Reactions

Think how you felt when you had an unexpected meeting with a German shepherd dog, narrowly missed a car wreck, or heard a knock at your door at 2 A.M. In moments like that you have three possible reactions as your body goes on automatic stress alert: fight, flight, or adapt. As an example, when you met the dog—you could (1) grab a stick to fight; (2) adapt by using Henry David Thoreau's advice, "When a dog runs at you, whistle for him"; or (3) run fast enough to earn a place in the *Guinness Book of World Records.* Survival might depend on choosing the right reaction.

All stress management requires some degree of choice. When harassment shows up in the workplace, you can fight to change conditions, resign, or accept a bad situation. A fight for improvement might bring needed changes or cause your dismissal. Flight may result in a better opportunity, but adaptation might condition you to become apathetic or careless. Every response forces stress-generated chemicals into your physical systems, and every choice causes some internal consequence.

It is crystal clear that the only appropriate response in some stress-producing situations is withdrawal. Sometimes parents find their teens' peer pressure at school so harmful that they relocate. Sometimes after all attempts fail at reconciliation, relationships deteriorate, so a person has to withdraw. Frequently, in difficult situations, flight choices like a change of setting or time off provide the only answer.

The only alternative on other occasions is to take an uncompromising stand. Many problems of society wait for someone to champion important causes. Good people cannot allow the world to get worse simply because they wish to avoid unpleasantness; the question is when and how to take a stand. The potential results of all stand-and-fight responses must be carefully evaluated because they can have such a far-reaching impact on both the outer and inner worlds.

What you do to other people, what you allow people to do to you, and what you think about circumstances determine what stress does to you. To lower stress, match your expectations to the realities of the environment. Once Martha Washington observed, "The greater part of our happiness or misery depends on our dispositions and not on our circumstances."[15] And she is right. You may not be able to control all stress-creating situations, but you do control the intensity of your feelings and responses. You can change. Shift work loads. Rewrite schedules. And when stress seems to be building, you may try a temporary dropout, find a change of scenery, or take a walk.

Your reactions determine the consequences stress can do to you.

Heart Exercise—Start a Cheering Section

Since tension feeds on fear of failure, a well-placed cheer by friend or family increases self-confidence and lowers stress. Though cheering sections are common in athletics all the way from Little League to the majors, the need to receive and give affirmation is grossly neglected in other areas of life. Consequently, an expression of praise possesses impact all out of proportion to the effort required to give it. For most people, praise is rare and criticism is common.

Everyone needs someone to cheer for them most of the time. Even highly competent people suffer self-doubt when they miss desired achievements. Less-gifted people feel stressed by a desperate need to keep trying. And beginners often crave encouragement to attempt things for the first time.

A pat on the back increases emotional energy and decreases tension.

Though everyone needs someone to recognize a victory in him, we mistakenly think a compliment will embarrass the praised person; so we either preface affirmations with apologies or withhold them altogether. I once met a person who summarized what most of us are reluctant to admit: "Even if I am embarrassed, I always remember praise because it makes me feel so good."

Think how encouragement torpedoes stress: compliments make students study harder; praise helps journalists write better; encouragement inspires instructors to teach more effectively; tender affirmation encourages a pastor to preach better; and applause makes athletes play harder. The biggest bonus of all, however, goes to the affirmer because it is impossible to be stressed while encouraging another. Everyone needs a cheer, and everyone needs to lead a cheer.

Heart Exercise—Reject Spiritual Competition

Contests hound us from the cradle to the grave in our get-ahead society. Babies are judged by when they walk, talk, or cut their first tooth, and some communities sponsor beauty contests for toddlers. Children are compared by grades, I.Q. scores, and height. Teens are pressured by athletics, drugs, and grades. Women judge each other by clothing brands, size of house, or behavior of children. And grown men compete with job titles, cars, or racquetball scores.

Comparisons cause stress at home, work, school, and in the marketplace; even inexpensive bowling and golf trophies negatively impact someone. Deep down, people keep asking, "Why can't I be as good as someone else in sports, art, or love?" Others revise the question, "Why don't I get the breaks, when I am as good as those who do?" These comparisons create unnecessary tensions through all the stages of life.

When the passion for competition stresses us, it is useful to consider the view of journalist Sydney J. Harris: "However diverse their talents, temperaments, and differences, all great achievers have one trait in common: they never bother to compare themselves with others, but are content to run their own race on their own terms."[16] Why not follow his idea by judging your spiritual development only by your own progress and potential?

God, because He has no favorites, has little interest in the comparisons we create for ourselves or others. To underscore the issue, Jesus recounted a story about two men who went to the Temple to pray. The Pharisee, well remembered for pompous piety, prayed, "God, I thank you that I am not like other men—robbers, evildoers, adulterers—or even like this tax collector. I fast twice a week and give a tenth of all I get." When his fellow worshiper, a tax collector, prayed, he would not even look up to heaven, but he beat his breast and cried, "God, have mercy on me, a sinner." After telling this incident, Jesus explained His position on spiritual competition: "I tell you that this man, rather than the other, went home justified before God" (Luke 18:11-14). Descendants of the Pharisee, still regrettably active, continue to sidetrack the personal spiritual formation of many conscientious disciples.

Comparisons, even self-inflicted ones, stymie spiritual growth for timid souls who believe their piety has to be like the most mature Christian they know. Others who seriously seek to connect practical life with faith are turned off by brash moral pygmies who claim to be spiritual giants by comparing themselves with others. How mistaken all of this is. Real saints never keep score, never contrast others unfavorably to themselves, and never brag of what they do or think. Authentic spiritual development always takes into account the fact that people differ in capacities, gifts, and inner needs. Emerson is right, "God enters by a private door into every individual."[17] Strugglers after God experience unspeakable peace when they no longer feel pressured to be a carbon copy of someone else but seek and find their own strategies for inner life development from God's amazingly rich smorgasbord of spiritual resources.

Realistically, there is no need to mimic admired saints because spiritual formation ripens according to individual distinctives. In fact, the spiritual masters like Francis of Assisi, St. John of the Cross, Evelyn Underhill, Rufus Jones, and Thomas Kelly had almost nothing in common except their determined quest to know the Lord more intimately. Consequently, it is useful to apply George MacDonald's view to our journey of faith: "I would rather be what God chose to make me, than the most glorious creature that I could think of. For to have been thought about—born in God's thoughts—and then made by God, is the dearest, grandest, most precious thing in all thinking."[18] This mysterious reality encourages every pilgrim to actualize his spiritual potential at his own speed.

Stress goes down when comparisons are eliminated and we seriously sing the prayer, "Oh, to be like Thee!"

Heart Exercise—Join the Towel Company

Servanthood, as it shouts from the pages of Scripture, is God's crowning pattern for finding fulfillment. Christ's teaching on the subject rings true to everything we know about human experience: "The greatest among you will be your servant" (Matt. 23:11). That means service is a gift we give to God, a helpful deed we do for a fellow human being, and a satisfying favor we do for ourselves.

Life is exhilarating when a great cause consumes us. This idea is captured by the English statesman James Bright: "You should link yourself to a great cause; you may never do the cause very much good, but the cause will do you a great deal of good."[19] This law of life, tested by thousands of serious Christian disciples, helps us understand that serving is a boomerang—the more we give, the more we receive. To give is to grow, and service saves us from the embarrassment of having God ask what we did with the benefits He gave us.

The towel company, though its objectives may seem hopelessly out-of-date, started in the heart of Jesus. To become a towel company member requires no stock purchases or well-connected recommendations. It simply starts by doing something for someone else in the name of Jesus. The servant of Christ, by such action, rejects a widely accepted notion that one individual cannot affect society. He can. In fact, one social scientist recently expressed the opinion that the quality of a whole culture can be changed when only 2 percent of the population have a new vision. The possibilities are mind-boggling.

In this towel company, a long history of people have

proven that selfless service is the most obvious characteristic of greatness. By example, our Lord taught that humble service leads to true nobility, and self-giving is the only path to fulfillment. This amazingly uncomplicated strategy for changing the world, meeting human need, and developing the individual Christian calls us simply to do whatever needs doing for Jesus' sake.

A possible destructive sidetrack must be avoided, however. Soon after they start, some disciples are duped into believing that position, power, and prestige are desirable ends in themselves. Regardless of their high-sounding descriptions, such worldly lusts never saved a soul, never brought a drug addict to health, never mended a broken family, never healed a sick child, or never helped a troubled teenager through turbulence. On the contrary, everyone can recall painful examples where status struggles wrecked churches, frustrated mission enterprises, crippled families, and destroyed dreams. Regrettably, vast energies that could have impacted the world for right were wasted chasing the fool's gold of control and notoriety. Control and notoriety for what? Or for whom?

Jesus offers an intriguing alternative when He asks His serious servants to spend themselves without thought of gain. Francis of Assisi proved that a fascinating life could be built on an amazing secret, "It is in giving that we receive."

A plaque displayed on the wall of a senior citizens' center amplifies the idea: "We wish to be involved, to seek, to quest, to adventure, to serve, to laugh at death. Let it come! We have lived!"[20] The authentic servant of Jesus, regardless of age or experience, knows he becomes rich by giving himself away.

Sarah Patton-Boyle, in a delightful description of putting her shoulder to another's wheel, defends the biblical ideal of the interrelatedness of service in the Body of Christ: "When we fail to contribute to the welfare of another, we separate ourselves from the circulatory system, the nerve impulses, and the energy of the whole. When we opt for non-service, we condemn ourselves to internal isolation."[21] Helping another diminishes personal stress at the same time as it forges bonds of relationship; each personal struggle seems easier when someone stands beside us.

Healing from jumbled emotions often starts with a simple decision to resign from the rat race that seeks to control others on the job, in the family, and in the church, and to serve others in the name of Jesus. Albert Day gives a formula for facing each fresh day without pressure: "Develop the habit of doing and being everything for His sake; loving people because He loves them; doing your work well because He loves excellence; being patient under provocation because that pleases and honors Him."[22] To the noble goal of being like the Master, members of the towel company find joy in giving creative imagination and honest toil.

Cardinal Newman describes the bedrock foundation of the towel company: "God has created me to do Him some definite service. He has committed some work to me which He has not committed to another . . . I am a link in a chain, a bond of connection between persons. He has not created me for naught. I shall do good. I shall do His work."[23]

A newsman, assuming the solution to the stress problem must be complex, quizzed an eminent psychiatrist about what the physician would do if he felt a personal emotional disorder coming on. The doctor's surprising reply fits the towel teachings of Jesus exactly: "I would close my office, go to the wrong side of the tracks, and help someone who is worse off than I am. And I would get well." This same idea appears in another form in the writings of Henri Nouwen, who after discussing the temporary usefulness of crying when trouble comes, says, "The ideal remains not to be concerned with yourself, not to cry, not to express all your emotions, but to forget your own problems, and do the work which calls for your attention and interest."[24] Stress erodes when the focus of life moves from self to others and to God.

Service in the towel company is devotion dressed in work clothes. Much more than another duty for a crowded schedule, servanthood is the God-given satisfaction that comes from doing a task for one of the Father's hurting people. Every effort done for another in Christ's name—an affirming note, a thoughtful deed, a caring phone call, a visit to a shut-in, an act of mercy, an encouraging hug, or a shared insight from Scripture—bonds giver, receiver, and God together. Then satisfaction and strength flow between all three parties. Servanthood transforms our efforts for others into fulfilling personal exhilaration.

Heart Recuperation—Renew Yourself

Well before 40, many give up creative ideas, reject new thoughts, and stop developing skills. "Too many times around the track; too few new challenges" is the way John W. Gardner describes it.[25] Then, for the remainder of their days these persons reside in self-made prisons where they feel walled in by familiar surroundings, dull relationships, and grim boredom. Though they do not experience fatal attacks of coronary failure or overexertion, they die by inches as hope dies and dreams crumble. Of them Fulton J. Sheen says, "The fires are going out; our salt is losing its savor."[26] In spite of their apathetic appearances, they are anxious and tense. What a waste for those whom God created to soar, to sing, and to adventure.

Deep within, a wistful regret chides this willingness to settle for deadly mediocrity. God challenges these faulty assumptions when He planted renewal in every heart just as surely as He put life into ugly tulip bulbs. Like crocuses push their way through late winter snowdrifts, the Father means for us to be called to arms by an insistent inner force that quizzes every acceptance of the status quo. Personal renewal fueled by spiritual disciples may be the only weapon strong enough to stand against dehumanization and secularization, so common in this period of history. But it is more than enough.

Renewal, however, must be seen for what it actually is. If viewed as just another duty, renewal will only lengthen our long list of responsibilities that compete for energy and attention. If that happens, the results will be zero. But if spiritual renewal is understood to offer meaning to life, most people may be ready to try.

The needed renewal requires that faith resources be applied to stress that originates from hostile criticism, work overload, encroachments on time, fatigue, invasion of privacy, and defeated dreams. Deadly mediocrity changes into renewal when we pray:

> *O Wind of God, come bend us, break us,*
> *Till humbly we confess our need;*
> *Then in Thy tenderness remake us,*
> *Revive, restore, for this we plead.*
> —BESSIE P. HEAD

Getting Your Heart in Shape

Getting and keeping in shape has become a billion-dollar business, a national obsession, and a way of life. To diagnostic, prescriptive, and surgical skills, the medical profession has added nutrition, prevention, and exercise to help us understand how to get fit and keep healthy. Now everyone knows wellness is desirable, possible, and to a large degree dependent on one's life-style. But what resources are available to prevent moral, spiritual, and intellectual heart trouble?

For spiritual development, God promises, "I will give you a new heart and put a new spirit in you" (Ezek. 36:26). Spirituality's powerfully effective prescriptions for interior wellness include prayer, worship, and Scripture, which enable us to function simply and joyfully in our pressure cooker environments. These remedies work when applied to all kinds of nerve-racking circumstances that are an inevitable part of modern life. These spiritual antibiotics destroy dreaded infections of worry and deadly viruses of tension that grow so silently in our unhealed wounds and overscheduled commitments. These immunizations prevent soul sickness by providing life-changing alternatives to our preoccupations with pleasure and comfort. Preventions as well as radical corrective surgery are offered.

Faith formation cures lots of moral heartbreaks with a wonderful blend of pure intention and divine empowerment.

Prayer and Scripture lessen many strains of stress that attack both the inner and outer world. For self-help Evelyn Underhill advises, "Remember you hold your body and nervous system in trust from God and you must treat His property well." To another she wrote, "Be one-tenth as kind to yourself as you were to me and you will do nicely."[27] When life is centered in Christ, the cardiac muscle experiences less wear and tear from secular activity at the same time as it grows strong with strenuous service. Vital faith strengthens the heart against ravaging breakdowns resulting from tension and strain. Spirituality provides holistic soundness at its best.

To clarify these issues, a final question must be considered: What for the individual is the desired outcome of spiritual development? Inasmuch as spiritual disciplines are not ends in themselves, their faithful practice is not proof of inner wellness any more than long hours of piano practice is evidence of a great musician. Keeping score or even breaking records of prayer, Bible reading, self-denial, or heroic service can increase stress and circumvent spiritual formation benefits by resurrecting self-centeredness and fueling pride. Even as the purpose of piano lessons and practice is to make beautiful music, the purpose of spiritual discipline is to break the stranglehold possessions, people, and self have on us. Albert E. Day clarifies the activity versus achievement issue: "It is not important how many times you have denied yourself but how truly you have detached yourself from yourself, set yourself free to think of God and love Him."[28] Practice and persistence, necessary as they may be, are only the process. The goal is quality living at its best. Heart wholeness builds on the believer's total commitment to keep the conditions of this requirement from Scripture: "Above all else, guard your heart, for it is the wellspring of life" (Prov. 4:23).

For healthy hearts and satisfying lives, we pray with Dag Hammarskjöld:
Give us
a pure heart that we may see Thee,
a humble heart that we may hear Thee,
a heart of love that we may serve Thee,
a heart of faith that we may live for Thee. Amen.[29]

Epilogue

I love spirituality because it
  exposes my whole life to faith;
  questions my motives and gives me inner vigor;
  revolutionizes my affections, so that I love what I once hated;
  corrects my nearsightedness and improves the hearing of my soul.

I love spirituality because it
  warns that possessions do not define life;
  shapes an accurate view of the world;
  shines light into the darkest night of my soul;
  encourages an honest modesty about myself.

I love spirituality because it
  energizes life with a melody, rhythm, and beat;
  creates a unique yearning for right living;
  changes behavior and makes faith real—even contagious;
  refocuses my thoughts about myself, my neighbor, and my God.

I love spirituality because it
  cultivates an awe for God, so I stand at full attention;
  demands that I relinquish foolish things that I once cherished;
  reminds me there is no courageous action without self-denial;
  chastens and affirms, crucifies and resurrects me.

I love spirituality because it
> harmonizes my deepest thoughts and warmest feelings;
> shows me God's road map to ultimate fulfillment;
> offers simplicity—the opposite of sophistication;
> forces me to suspect my entrenched assumptions about myself.

I love spirituality because it
> reveals how close God is to me—as close as my soul;
> makes me a better parent, a better mate, and a better person;
> calls me to a lifelong imitation of Christ;
> provides wholeness, wellness, and holiness too.

Notes

Chapter 1

1. Henri J. M. Nouwen, *Reaching Out* (Garden City, N.Y.: Doubleday and Co., 1966), 116.
2. Paul R. Clancy, *Just a Country Lawyer* (Bloomington, Ind.: Indiana University Press, 1974), 54.
3. Paula Ripple, *Growing Strong in Broken Places* (Notre Dame, Ind.: Ave Maria Press, 1986), 53.
4. Rueben P. Job and Norman Shawchuck, *A Guide to Prayer for Ministers and Other Servants* (Nashville: Upper Room, 1983), 274.
5. Ernest Holmes, *This Thing Called Life* (New York: Dodd, Mead, and Co., 1943), 32.
6. Albert Edward Day, *An Autobiography of Prayer* (Nashville: Upper Room, 1952), 18.
7. Kenneth Leech, *True Prayer* (San Francisco: Harper and Row, 1980), 68.
8. Urban T. Holmes, *A History of Christian Spirituality* (Minneapolis: Seabury Press, 1980), 90.
9. Malcolm Muggeridge, *Confessions of a Twentieth Century Pilgrim* (San Francisco: Harper and Row, 1988), 34.
10. Paul Tournier, *Creative Suffering* (San Francisco: Harper and Row, 1981), 44.
11. Interview, *Denver Post,* Sept. 13, 1986, sec. F, 11.
12. Dee Danner Barwick, ed., *A Treasury of Days* (Norwalk, Conn.: Reader's Digest Books, 1983), 15.
13. Muggeridge, *Confessions,* 17.
14. Brother Lawrence, *The Practice of the Presence of God* (Grand Rapids: Baker Book House, 1975), 36-37.
15. Perry D. LeFevre, *The Prayers of Kierkegaard* (Chicago: University of Chicago Press, 1956), 36.
16. Thomas Merton, *Thoughts on Solitude* (New York: Farrar, Straus, and Giroux, 1958).
17. Muggeridge, *Confessions,* 13.
18. John Powell, S.J., poster (Allen, Tex.: Argus Communications, n.d.).

Chapter 2

1. Holmes, *A History of Christian Spirituality*, 154.
2. Alice Munro, "Points to Ponder," *Reader's Digest*, June 1990, 52; from *The Progress of Love* (New York: Knopf, n.d.).
3. Dean Inge, *Studies in English Mystics* (New York: Dutton, 1906), 35.
4. Bob Benson and Michael Benson, *Disciplines for the Inner Life* (Waco, Tex.: Word Books, Publisher, 1985), 31.
5. Nathan O. Hatch, "Yesterday, the Key That Unlocks Today," *Christianity Today*, August 5, 1983, 18.
6. John Roger and Peter McWilliams, *Life* (Los Angeles: Prelude Press, 1990), 218.
7. Robert Lawrence Ottley, *Studies in the Beginning Confessions of Augustine* (London: R. Scott, 1919), 2.
8. Jean M. Bloomquist, "Of Seeds and Suffering," *Weavings* 4, no. 3 (May/June 1989): 10.
9. Francis Fénelon, *Christian Perfection* (Minneapolis: Bethany, 1976), 43-44.
10. Joan W. Brown, *Joy in His Presence* (Minneapolis: World Wide Publications, 1982), May 25.
11. Evelyn Underhill, *The Spiritual Life* (New York: Harper and Row, n.d.), 36-38.
12. Frederick Buechner, *Now and Then* (San Francisco: Harper and Row, 1983), 87.
13. Thomas R. Kelly, *A Testament of Devotion* (New York: Harper and Brothers Publishers, 1941), 29.
14. Paul Scherer, *Love Is a Spendthrift* (New York: Harper and Brothers Publishers, 1961), 122.
15. Ibid., 184.
16. Jurgen Moltmann, *The Passion for Life* (Philadelphia: Fortress Press, 1977), 39.
17. Thomas P. McDonnell, ed., *A Thomas Merton Reader* (Garden City, N.Y.: Image Books, 1985), 427.
18. Robert Inchuasti, "Interpreting Mother Teresa," *Christian Century*, Oct. 16, 1985, 918.

Chapter 3

1. Claudia Wallis, "Stress: Can We Cope?" *Time*, June 6, 1983, 48.
2. P. W. Buffington, "An Anti-Stress Survival Kit," *Sky Magazine*, April 1983, 85.

3. Herbert J. Freudenberger, *Burnout* (New York: Bantam Books, 1980), 15.
4. Robert F. Norneau, *There Is a Season* (Englewood, N.J.: Prentice-Hall, 1984), 76.
5. Henri J. M. Nouwen, *Intimacy* (San Francisco: Harper and Row, 1959), 111.
6. Arthur M. Schlesinger, Jr., *Robert Kennedy and His Times*, vol. 2 (Boston: Houghton Mifflin Co., 1978), 811.
7. Thomas P. McDonnell, ed., *Through the Year with Thomas Merton* (Garden City, N.Y.: Image Books, 1985), 40.
8. Pat McKeown, "Businesses Serious About Reducing Stress," *Boca Raton (Fla.) News*, Oct. 17, 1982, sec. D, 2.
9. Ibid.
10. Jane E. Brody, "Cure Tension Pain; Just Learn to Relax," *Fort Lauderdale (Fla.) News*, May 20, 1982, sec. D, 1-2.
11. *New York Daily News*, Oct. 10, 1983.
12. Reinhold Niebuhr, *Parting the Waters* (New York: Touchstone, 1988), 83.
13. Edmund Spencer, *As a Man Thinketh* (Kansas City: Hallmark Books, 1968), 21.
14. Robert S. Eliot and Dennis L. Breo, *Is It Worth Dying For?* (New York: Bantam Books, 1989), 38.
15. McDonnell, *Through the Year with Thomas Merton*, 63.
16. *Fort Lauderdale (Fla.) Sun-Sentinel*, Aug. 2, 1990, 16.
17. Lloyd J. Ogilvie, *Making Stress Work for You* (Waco, Tex.: Word, 1984), 206.

Chapter 4

1. Judith C. Lechman, *The Spirituality of Gentleness* (San Francisco: Harper and Row, 1987), 40.
2. Dag Hammarskjöld, *Markings* (New York: Knopf, 1964), 15.
3. Ted Delaney, "High-tech's High Tool," *Denver Post*, Dec. 8, 1985, sec. G, 1.
4. Ibid.
5. Michael Dougan, "Success Complicated Life; Wilson Through with Acting," *Colorado Springs Gazette Telegraph*, Sept. 15, 1985.
6. C. S. Lewis, *George MacDonald: An Anthology* (New York: Macmillan Co., 1986), 34.
7. Walt Menninger, "Stress: You Can Learn to Make It Beneficial," *Boca Raton News*, Jan. 22, 1982, sec. A, 10.

8. A. J. Buckingham, "In One Day," *Fort Lauderdale News*, Dec. 23, 1984, sec. G, 1.
9. "November Almanac," *Atlantic*, November 1986, 20.
10. George MacDonald, *Diary of an Old Soul* (Minneapolis: Augsburg Press, 1975), 52.
11. Lechman, *Spirituality of Gentleness*, 55.
12. Richard Lovelace, *Dynamics of Spiritual Life* (Downers Grove, Ill.: InterVarsity Press, 1979), 92.
13. Rueben P. Job and Norman Shawchuck, *A Guide to Prayer for Ministers and Other Servants* (Nashville: Upper Room, 1983), 92.
14. T. S. Eliot, *Choices from the Rock: Collected Poems, 1909-1935*, as quoted by Don Postema, *Space for God* (Grand Rapids: Bible Way, 1983), 15.
15. Frank C. Laubach, *Learning the Vocabulary of God* (Nashville: Upper Room, 1956), 42.

Chapter 5

1. Stephen R. Covey, *The Divine Center* (Salt Lake City: Bookcraft, 1982), 69.
2. Fulton J. Sheen, *On Being Human* (New York: Image Books, 1983), 312.
3. Thomas R. Kelly, *A Testament of Devotion* (New York: Harper and Brothers Publisher, 1941), 115-16.
4. Robert Raines, *Creative Brooding* (New York: Macmillan Co., 1966), 112.
5. Thomas R. Kelly, *The Eternal Promise* (London: Hodder and Stoughton, 1966), 48.
6. Mother Teresa, *A Gift from God* (San Francisco: Harper and Row, 1974), 75.
7. George Appleton, ed., *The Oxford Book of Prayer* (London: Oxford University Press, 1985), 7.
8. Calvin Miller, *A Hunger for Meaning* (Downers Grove, Ill.: InterVarsity Press, 1984), 40.
9. Vance Havner, *Day by Day* (Grand Rapids: Baker Book House, 1953), 77.
10. Kelly, 23.
11. Frank C. Laubach, *Letters by a Modern Mystic* (Westwood, N.J.: Fleming H. Revell, 1937), 29.
12. Albert E. Day, *Discipline and Discovery* (Nashville: Upper Room, 1977), 100.
13. Kelly, 47.

14. R. Huelsman, *Intimacy with Jesus* (Mahwah, N.J.: Paulist Press, 1985), 73.
15. Glenn Clark, "I Will Lift Up My Eyes," quoted in *A Guide to Prayer for Ministers and Other Servants* (Nashville: Upper Room, 1983), 93.

Chapter 6

1. Paul Goodman, *Little Prayers and Finite Experience* (New York: Harper and Row, 1972), 16.
2. James Earl Massey, *Spiritual Disciplines* (Grand Rapids: Francis Asbury Press, 1985), 108.
3. Al Bryant, comp., *New Every Morning* (Waco, Tex.: Word Books, 1985), 90.
4. McDonnell, *Through the Year with Thomas Merton*, 163.
5. Christopher Carstens and William P. Mahedy, *Right Here, Right Now* (New York: Ballantine Books, 1985), 58.
6. Kenneth W. Osbeck, *101 Hymn Stories* (Grand Rapids: Kregel Publications, 1982), foreword.
7. Charles M. Sell, *Transitions* (Chicago: Moody Press, 1985), x, xxi.
8. *Reader's Digest*, June 1990, 52.

Chapter 7

1. Michael Quoist, *Prayers of Life* (Philadelphia: Westminster Press, 1967), 77.
2. Kenneth L. Gibble, "Listening to My Life: An Interview with Frederick Buechner," *Christianity Today*, Nov. 16, 1983.
3. James Dent, *Charleston (W.Va.) Gazette*, as quoted in *Reader's Digest*, July 1987, 143.
4. Milo Arnold, *Adventure of Christian Ministry* (Kansas City: Beacon Hill Press of Kansas City, 1967), 37.
5. *Colorado Springs Gazette Telegraph*, Jan. 29, 1987, sec. B, 13.
6. Barwick, *A Treasury of Days*, 41.
7. Eugene Kennedy, *A Time for Being Human* (New York: Simon and Schuster, 1977), 5.
8. James B. Simpson, *Simpson's Contemporary Quotations* (Boston: Houghton Mifflin Co., 1988), 240.
9. Barwick, *A Treasury of Days*, 83.
10. Eliot and Breo, *Is It Worth Dying For?* 115.
11. Benson and Benson, *Disciplines for the Inner Life*, 166.

12. Robert Wood, *A Thirty-Day Experiment in Prayer* (Nashville: Upper Room, 1977), 30.
13. Bob Benson, *See You at the House* (Nashville: Generoux, 1986), 53.
14. James C. Fenhagen, *Invitation to Holiness* (San Francisco: Harper and Row, 1985), 57.
15. Benson and Benson, *Disciplines for the Inner Life*, 279.
16. Frederick Buechner, *Godric* (New York: Atheneum, 1981), 142.
17. Carstens and Mahedy, *Right Here, Right Now*, 11.
18. Ibid., 12.
19. Francis Fénelon, *Christian Perfection* (Minneapolis: Bethany House, 1976), 29.
20. Frederick Buechner, *Wishful Thinking* (New York: Harper and Row, 1973), 85.
21. Douglas Rhymes, *Prayer in the Secular City* (Philadelphia: Westminster Press, 1967), 15.
22. Richard Bach, "The Bridge Across Forever," *Reader's Digest*, April 1990, 51.
23. Frederick Buechner, *Now and Then* (New York: Harper and Row, 1983), 87.
24. Barwick, *A Treasury of Days*, 609.
25. Robert J. Hastings, "The Station," as quoted by Ann Landers, *Denver Post*, Aug. 9, 1986, sec. B, 8.
26. John Henry Jowett, *Yet Another Day* (Westwood, N.J.: Fleming H. Revell, 1905), October 21.
27. *Reader's Digest*, March 1990, 150.
28. R. Alec Mackenzie, *Time Trap* (New York: ACACOM, 1972), 49.
29. Ann Landers, *Denver Post*, Aug. 9, 1986.
30. Jean de Caussade, *Abandonment*, as quoted by Thomas E. Clarke, S.J., "Never a Dull Moment," *Weavings* 2, no. 3 (May/June 1987): 18.
31. Sarah Patton-Boyle, *The Desert Blooms* (Nashville: Abingdon Press, 1983), 43.
32. *Herald of Holiness*, Dec. 27, 1967, 2.
33. John W. Gardner, *On Leadership* (New York: Free Press, 1990), 199.
34. Ibid., 135.

Chapter 8

1. "Graffiti," *Colorado Springs Gazette Telegraph*, Apr. 24, 1987.

2. As quoted by Diana C. Austin, *Christian Ministry*, September 1986, 30.
3. *Colorado Springs Gazette Telegraph*, Aug. 13, 1985, sec. C, 5.
4. Vernon Grounds, "Establishing a Faith Fellowship," *Ministries Library Journal* 3:7.
5. "Graffiti," *Colorado Springs Gazette Telegraph*, Mar. 12, 1987.
6. John Mogabgab, "Editorial Introduction," *Weavings* 1 (November/December 1986): 2.
7. *Weavings* 2 (July/August, 1987): 3.
8. Albert Schweitzer, *Memories of Childhood and Youth* (New York: Macmillan Co., 1931), 64.
9. Bob Benson, *See You at the House*, 183.
10. Halford E. Luccock, *Treasury of Illustrations* (Nashville: Abingdon, 1962), 14.
11. Susan M. Campbell, *The Couple's Journey* (San Luis Obispo, Calif.: Impact Books, 1980), 132.
12. Oswald Chambers, *Still Higher for His Highest* (Grand Rapids: Zondervan, 1970), 15.
13. Helen Hayes, "Weekend," *USA Today*, Oct. 5, 1986, 17.
14. Peter DeVries, *Forbes*, June 30, 1986, 160.
15. Kathy Coffey, "With Baby and Briefcase," *Denver Post*, Aug. 11, 1985.
16. *Denver Post*, Jan. 27, 1987, sec. G, 4.
17. *Denver Post*, Aug. 25, 1986, sec. A, 2.
18. John Powell, *Unconditional Love* (Allen, Tex.: Argus Communications, 1978), 62.
19. Grounds, "Establishing a Faith Fellowship," 6.
20. Lawrence J. Crabb, Jr., and Dan B. Allender, *Encouragement, the Key to Caring* (Grand Rapids: Zondervan, 1984), 11.
21. Thomas Merton, *The Wisdom of the Desert* (New York: New Directions, 1960), 71.
22. Ted Engstrom, *The Fine Art of Friendship* (Nashville: Thomas Nelson, 1985), 61.
23. *Colorado Springs Gazette Telegraph*, Aug. 1, 1986.

Chapter 9

1. Day, *An Autobiography of Prayer*, 124.
2. Marjorie J. Thompson, "To Do Justice," *Weavings* 1 (November-December 1986): 29.
3. Halford E. Luccock, *365 Windows* (Nashville: Abingdon Press, 1955), 229.

4. Douglas V. Steer, ed., *Quaker Spirituality* (New York: Paulist Press, 1984), 4.
5. Scherer, *Love Is a Spendthrift*, 101.
6. Benson and Benson, *Disciplines for the Inner Life*, 37.
7. Muggeridge, *Confessions*, 67.
8. George Buttrick, *Prayer* (Nashville: Abingdon Press, 1942), 112.
9. Ibid., 107.
10. Reference not available.
11. Frank C. Laubach, *Prayer, the Mightiest Force in the World* (Westwood, N.J.: Fleming H. Revell Co., 1949), 78.
12. Harry E. Fosdick, *The Meaning of Prayer* (Nashville: Abingdon, 1982), 6.
13. Ibid., 9.
14. Ibid., 78.
15. Bryant, *New Every Morning*, 11.
16. Lawrence, *The Practice of the Presence of God*, 11.
17. Maxie Dunnam, *The Workbook of Intercessory Prayer* (Nashville: Upper Room, 1979), 22.
18. Fosdick, *The Meaning of Prayer*, 116.
19. Victor Hugo, "Quotable Quotes," *Reader's Digest*, n.d., 171.
20. Miller, *A Hunger for Meaning*, 75.
21. Horace Walpole, letter to Sir Horace Mann, December 31, 1769, quoted in *The International Thesaurus of Quotations*, ed. Rhoda Tripp (New York: Harper and Row, 1970), 711.
22. Ripple, *Growing Strong in Broken Places*, 165.
23. Richard Foster, *Celebration of Discipline* (San Francisco: Harper and Row, 1978), 90.
24. Mary Strong, *Letters of the Scattered Brotherhood* (New York: Harper and Row, 1948), 8.
25. Robert Larranaga, *Calling It a Day* (San Francisco: Harper and Row, 1990), Dec. 28.
26. Source unknown.
27. *Colorado Springs Gazette Telegraph*, Aug. 8, 1987, sec. D, 8.
28. Steve Harper, *Devotional Life in the Wesleyan Tradition* (Nashville: Upper Room, 1983), 22.
29. Bob Benson, *See You at the House*, 95.

Chapter 10

1. Scherer, *Love Is a Spendthrift*, 79.
2. Reference unavailable.

3. William Johnston, *Christian Mysticism Today,* as quoted by Benson and Benson, *Disciplines for the Inner Life,* 91.
4. *Newsweek,* Dec. 17, 1982, 45.
5. Luccock, *365 Windows,* 120.
6. Laubach, *Prayer,* 97.
7. Buechner, *Now and Then,* 9.
8. Terry Hall, *Getting More from Your Bible* (Wheaton, Ill.: Victor Books, 1984), 42-43.
9. James Z. Nettinga, *Bible Society Record,* January 1968.
10. Hall, *Getting More from Your Bible,* 147.
11. William Barclay, *Fishers of Men* (Philadelphia: Westminster Press, 1966), 17-18.

Chapter 11

1. Scherer, *Love Is a Spendthrift,* 3.
2. Martin Luther King, "Answer to a Perplexing Question," in *20 Centuries of Great Preaching,* vol. 12 (Waco, Tex.: Word Books, Publisher, 1971), 371.
3. Chambers, *Still Higher for His Highest,* 18.
4. E. Stanley Jones, *Good News Magazine,* February 1986, 4.
5. Brown, *Joy in His Presence,* May 26.
6. John W. Gardner, *Self-renewal* (New York: W. W. Norton and Co., 1981), 13.
7. Karen Casey and Martha Vanceburg, *The Promise of a New Day* (New York: Winston Press, 1983), Jan. 28.
8. McDonnell, *Through the Year with Thomas Merton,* 68.
9. *Hymns for the Family of God,* 484.
10. Dominique Lapierre, *City of Joy* (New York: Winston Press, 1986), 233.
11. McDonnell, *Through the Year with Thomas Merton,* 64.
12. Amy E. Dean, *Night Light* (New York: Winston Press, 1986), Oct. 29.
13. John Kirk, *The Mother of the Wesleys* (London: Jarrold and Sons, 1864), 144.
14. McDonnell, *Through the Year with Thomas Merton,* 153.
15. Casey and Vanceburg, *The Promise of a New Day,* Aug. 25.
16. Barwick, *A Treasury of Days,* 41.
17. Fosdick, *The Meaning of Prayer,* 36.
18. Rolland Hein, ed., *The World of George MacDonald* (Wheaton, Ill.: Harold Shaw Publishers, 1978), 44.
19. Edward S. Mann, *Linked to a Cause* (Kansas City: Pedestal Press, 1986), preface.

20. Kim Williams, *Book of Uncommon Sense* (New York: Fawcett, 1987), 148.
21. Sarah-Patton Boyle, *The Desert Blooms*, 166.
22. Day, *Discipline and Discovery*, 124.
23. Cardinal Newman, *A Meditation by Cardinal Newman*, n.d.
24. Nouwen, *Intimacy*, 95.
25. Gardner, *On Leadership*, 133.
26. Sheen, *On Being Human*, 315.
27. Day, *Discipline and Discovery*, 136.
28. Ibid., 131.
29. *Hymns for the Family of God*, 610.